The
ART & CRAFT
of
PAPER

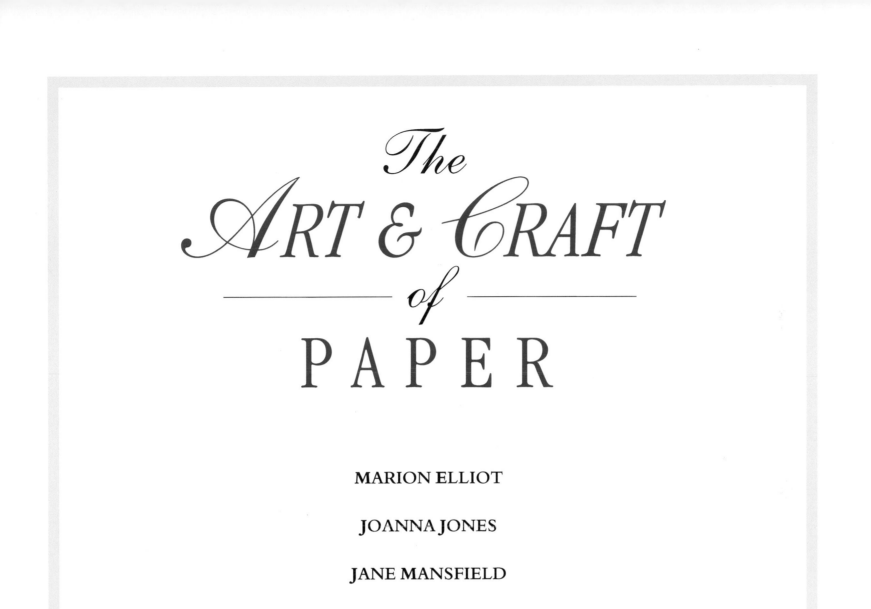

The
ART & CRAFT
of
PAPER

MARION ELLIOT

JOANNA JONES

JANE MANSFIELD

SOLVEIG STONE

MEREHURST

Published in 1995 by Merehurst Limited, Ferry House
51–57 Lacy Road, Putney, London SW15 1PR

Copyright © Merehurst Limited 1995
Reprinted 1996

ISBN 1–85391–437–1

A catalogue record of this book is available from the British
Library.

Edited by **Heather Dewhurst**
Designed by **Maggie Aldred**
Photography by **Jon Bouchier** (all photographs except those
on pp 45, 53, 56–59) and **Di Lewis** 53, 56–59)
Styling by **Joanna Jones** (pp 77–109)

Typeset by J&L Composition Ltd

Colour separation printing and binding
by Toppan, Singapore

Contents

Introduction

Paper is an extremely versatile medium, offering tremendous scope for creativity. *The Art & Craft of Paper* provides an inspirational introduction to paper and explores different ways of using it. You will learn how easy it is to make your own paper, marble on paper, decorate items with découpage, and, finally, recycle waste paper to make objects from papier mâché.

One of the oldest of all crafts, papermaking is now enjoying a revival. With the endless range of materials you can add to paper for decoration and texture, beautiful handmade paper can be produced for little cost and with relatively little experience. The section on handmade paper introduces the reader to this fascinating ancient craft and sets out the techniques of making pulp, forming and pressing sheets, drying paper and creating laminated sheets.

The section on marbling introduces the reader to this simple but stunningly effective technique and shows how to create beautiful marbled patterns – there are endless combinations of colour and pattern that can be achieved. Marbling is easy to do from home, and needs little in the way of equipment, which makes it the ideal craft for the complete beginner.

Nor is any experience needed for the delightful and highly popular craft of découpage, which is essentially decorating with cut-out paper images to achieve a finish that looks hand-painted. This section offers advice on choosing a suitable piece for decorating, preparing surfaces and applying varnishes, and gives suggestions on how to choose the right paper and build up a design.

Papier mâché, the final section of the book, demonstrates the ideal way to recycle waste paper. This immensely enjoyable craft is simple to do and can produce amazing results, even for the complete novice. This section sets out the techniques of layering paper strips over moulds, making armatures from card and adding pulp decoration.

Included in each section of the book are several delightful projects to make using the techniques of each paper craft. These range from a charming notebook made using handmade paper, an elegant marbled candleshade, a hat box decorated with découpage, and a whimsical papier mâché clock. So, to discover and enjoy the delights of papermaking, marbling, découpage and papier mâché, read on.

Handmade Paper

Papermaking is a subtle art. Paper is an ephemeral material that we take so much for granted, so accustomed are we to it. Yet it has not always been so. So what is paper?

Paper is derived from the cellulose within plants. This is broken down into individual fibres which have been intentionally damaged so that they will later bond together better. This process is known as 'fibrilation'. These fibres are then re-formed into sheets, whose strength is obtained by the interlocking of the damaged fibres.

The first true fibrilated paper was made in China in 105AD from a mixture of old rags, fishing nets, hemp and bark. Fabrication of the paper was kept a closely guarded secret, but inevitably the information leaked out and the secret of papermaking travelled further west, following the lines of trade. It was not until the 1480s that papermaking was first practised in Britain. Papermakers experimented with their local fauna wherever they happened to be worldwide. This resulted in Japanese papermakers traditionally using kozo, gampi and mitsumata; hemp, flax and esparto grass were favoured elsewhere, but in Europe, cotton and linen rags became the main source.

By the 1870s the making of 100 per cent wood pulp paper in volume on fully automated machines was becoming the norm, leaving low volume 'specialist' papers to be made by hand. The decline in the number of hand papermakers has continued consistently until relatively recently, when mainly artists have turned back to this source due to their dissatisfaction with mechanically produced papers.

The vast papermaking industry of today now spreads across much of the globe, often processing the wood from one continent into paper in another and it bears little resemblance to the small-scale production of its origin. During its time, paper has been made into products as diverse as coffins, cloth, currency, building materials, unwanted mail shots and vast quantities of toilet tissue; yet, it also feeds the computers of today.

I have found something both restful and timeless in the sound of the dripping water and the rhythm of the papermaking process. I trust that you too will experience a part of that delight when you become a link in the chain that leads through time.

▶ *A resurgence of interest in papermaking has led to a wide range of exciting uses for handmade paper.*

Equipment and Techniques

Most of the equipment that you will need to start papermaking is probably already in your home, the likely exception being the mould and deckle, which are neither expensive nor difficult to make. The basic techniques of papermaking are simple to grasp and, once equipped with them, you will have a whole new range of texture at your fingertips.

Equipment and materials

PAPERMAKING IS A WET BUSINESS, SO YOU NEED TO work where water can drain away. You also need enough space for your tank, felts, sheets and wet pulp. Once you have established these requirements, you can turn to the more specific materials listed below.

TANK/VAT

You will need a tank/vat to hold the mix of water and fibres from which the paper is made. The size of the largest sheet of paper that you will be able to make will be determined by the wooden frames that you have. These in their turn, should fit comfortably into your tank/vat when being held firmly by your hands, one on either side. A4 is a bit tight in most washing-up bowls, but a baby bath or an undrilled garden planter which are available in larger sizes do the job nicely. Failing that, you could work directly into a sink, but be careful not to allow too much pulp to go down the drain . . . especially if you have a drainage problem.

THE WOODEN FRAMES – 'MOULD AND DECKLE'

A sheet of paper is made on a wooden frame called a mould. The deckle is the removable wooden frame that sits on the mould to define the paper edge. Making the mould and deckle is

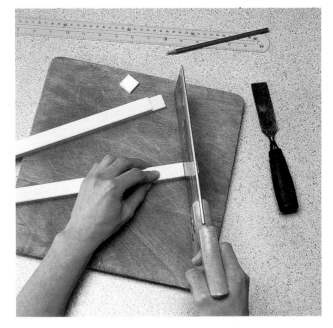

▲ *To make a mould and deckle, saw halfway through the depth of both ends of the eight pieces of wood and chisel out the end pieces.*

▶ *Place the two frames together and drill two holes through each of the overlapping corner pieces. Glue the wood together and secure with screws.*

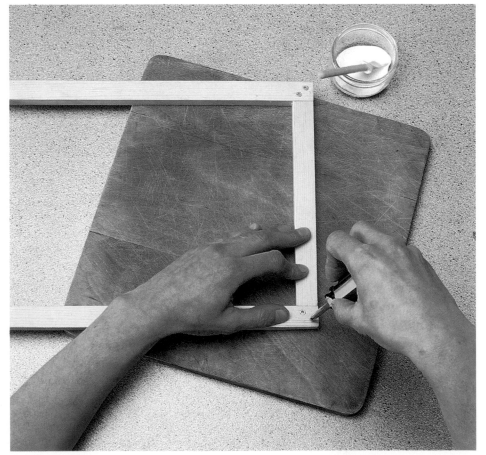

the most fiddly and least rewarding part of paper-making, but it is worth taking some time over, and with care, your mould and deckle could last you many years. (It is possible to buy a mould and deckle ready made, often in papermaking kits. If you would rather buy one, make sure that the mesh is tight.)

Small sheets of paper are easier to make, and use less pulp, so I recommend starting on A5 (148 × 210mm), certainly no larger than A4 (210 × 297mm). The projects in this book could be achieved using an A4 mould, but check that your intended mould and deckle size fits comfortably into your intended vat, with sufficient space for your hands. You may be fortunate enough to find two strong wooden picture frames securely pinned at their corners, in which case just oil or

varnish them as described below. Alternatively you may need to make them yourself.

Making a mould and deckle To make a set you will need a saw, a ruler, a pen/pencil, screws, waterproof wood glue, a hammer and a chisel. Hard wood is preferable for the job, but it is more expensive and soft wood would suffice. Choose a section of wood measuring approximately 1.5 × 1.5cm ($\frac{5}{8}$ × $\frac{5}{8}$in); I find the maximum I can comfortably hold is 2.5cm × 12mm (1 × $\frac{1}{2}$in). Bear in mind that whichever section you choose it should feel comfortable in your hands when you have two pieces, one on top of the other. The most secure yet simple joint to make is a halving joint; to do this you will need to cut the wood allowing for the joining of that piece to two others, top and bottom, so, for a complete mould and deckle set you will need:

> 4 pieces of wood at the length of your sheet plus 2 wood widths
> 4 pieces of wood at the width of your sheet plus 2 wood widths

Mark a line at both ends showing the width of the wood. Saw halfway through the depth of the wood at the line at both ends. Using a hammer and chisel, chisel downwards at the end until a 'bite' has come out. Pare off any wood that will prevent a good union. Do this to each of your eight pieces of wood.

Place together the two frames. Drill two holes through the overlapping corner pieces to about three-quarters of their total depth. Glue the wood together and secure the joints by screwing in screws of the correct length (three-quarters of the total wood depth). Let the glue dry, then apply two coats of wood oil or polyurethane varnish and allow it to dry thoroughly. Leave one frame as it is – this is the deckle.

For the mould you will need some net curtain or wire. If using net, a fairly open gauge nylon/terylene net with no obvious pattern is preferable.

▼ *Attach the net to the mould with drawing pins around each side of the frame, keeping the net taut. Cut off the spare net.*

Wire is more difficult to obtain and to handle, but it is harder wearing and on larger sizes it is easier to form sheets of even thickness. You need a wire that will not rust, for example stainless steel, aluminium, or a plastic-coated mild steel wire with 18–22 wires per inch. If you intend to make a mould and deckle for larger sheets than A4, you will definitely need a wire mesh.

Cut the net/wire at least 10cm (4in) larger in both directions than your mould size. Lay the net/wire onto a flat surface and place the mould on top. Attach the net/wire securely to one long side of the mould by inserting drawing pins or staples into the uppermost surface, keeping the net/wire taut on that side. The net will stretch when it is wet, so from now on pull it as tight as you can, without ripping it! The wire, too, needs to be taut. Now secure the opposite edge, starting at the centre. Finally, secure the two remaining short ends. Cut off the spare net/wire. To prevent paper fibres from lodging under the loose edge where it is difficult to clean, you may if you wish tape down the loose edge with brown parcel tape (in the process you will cover the drawing pins/staples). Overtape the corners. Do not get any tape onto the area that will be forming the sheet.

OLD BLANKETS/'FELTS'

These are needed for couching the newly made sheets of paper. Old blankets, towels or nappies need to be cut into pieces approximately 10cm (4in) larger than the largest sheet you intend to make (they can be folded for smaller sheets). If you do not have any of the above, I have seen newspaper wads do a reasonably efficient job. The more felts you have, the greater the pile of papers you will be able to make at a time without having to stop – but you will need at least 12 to get started.

BOARDS

To carry and press your wet pieces of paper, you will need two wooden boards. Ideally, they should be slightly larger than your felts – say an extra 2.5cm (1in) in each direction – but any flat piece of wood larger than your felt will do.

VISCOSE CLOTHS/NAPPY LINERS

Traditionally papermakers worked directly onto felts, but when working with various dyes it is much easier if you protect your felts. It is also easier to get rid of any mistakes from these smooth surfaces than that of a felt. Nappy liners are fine for small sheet sizes, and have the advantage of being transparent, but they do not wear too well. Viscose kitchen cloths with small orange, blue or green square patterns running in diagonals across them wear well and will accommodate up to A4 in size. (Don't buy similar products with diamond patterns and small holes in them – they are not as effective.) If you go any larger than A4, plain cotton or polycotton mixes do the job, but be careful of fraying edges.

LIQUIDIZER

A kitchen liquidizer is extremely useful for making paper pulp. Food processors do not seem to beat the pulp up as quickly or quite as thoroughly, but they do a satisfactory job. Alternatively, you are looking at a bucket and a potato masher, aided in later stages by a food mixer.

PULP INGREDIENTS

Old envelopes, drawings, drawing paper, bills, wrapping paper, paper bags and computer print-out paper are all ideal ingredients for pulp. You could also try flimsier materials, such as egg cartons, tissues, and kitchen towels. The quality of what you put in will be reflected in what you get out and, for this reason, I avoid using newsprint and glossy magazines. The former makes everything filthy and the latter contains very little paper fibre, being mostly comprised of china clay which is responsible for its glossy smooth surface. You may prefer to work with only clean paper and add colouring elements of your choice, for you will find that even a small amount of print on your original paper is enough to tint the whole batch.

PULP COLOURING AGENTS

To alter the colour of your pulp, experiment by adding powdered or liquid tempera colours and acrylics, cold water dyes, and even different concentrations of tea and coffee.

SIZE

It is sometimes necessary to size the paper to give it a coating which prevents it absorbing ink like blotting paper. The simplest sizes to use are wallpaper paste and PVA glue (see page 26).

PLANT MATERIAL

It is possible to make paper purely from plants, for which you will need plant material that is fibrous but not woody, such as bamboo leaves. Unfortunately, making pure plant paper is beyond the scope of this book.

COTTON LINTERS

Use these as an alternative to recycled papers for making pulp. They come in large, thick, slightly creamy coloured sheets and are comprised of fibres from the cotton plant left after the ginning operation. Paper made from cotton linters is soft and much stronger than recycled wood paper; however, the drawback is that cotton linters can be difficult to obtain.

▶ *To make paper pulp, you can use clean paper, cotton linters, old waste paper, envelopes, computer print-out paper, and even fibrous plant material.*

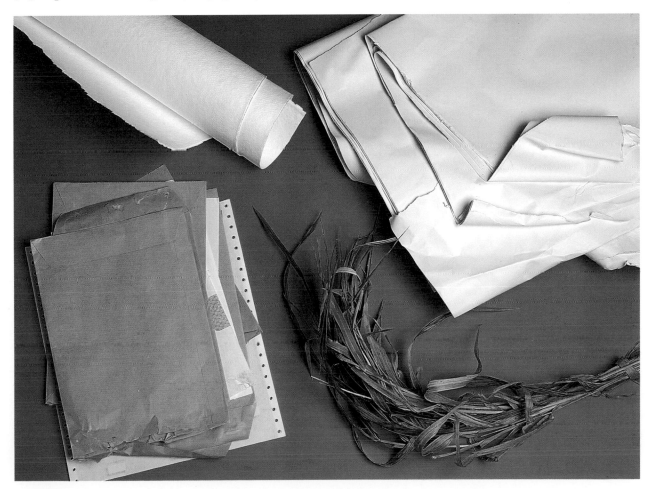

Basic techniques

THERE ARE SEVERAL ADVANTAGES TO A BEGINNER TO papermaking of using a recycled paper base, namely its availability, relative cheapness and ease of preparation. The traditional method of preparing the pulp described below, however, holds good for other pulps, for example cotton linters or pure plant – though each pulp prepared from different sources will have slightly different characteristics to work with.

A word of warning before you begin – papermaking is a wet business; both you and the surfaces that you work on, including the floor, are likely to get, at the least, splashed. So it is advisable to wear an apron and protect your surfaces with plastic sheeting.

PREPARING THE PULP

Tear the pieces of your chosen paper into 2.5–5cm (1–2in) squares. Leave to soak overnight in cold water. If you are in a hurry, soak the pieces in hot water for as long as you can, so that the paper is wet all the way through. Just one bucket of torn paper (prior to the wetting, and consequent

compacting taking place), will probably be ample to start with.

Place the soaked pieces of paper into a liquidizer goblet to a capacity of approximately one-eighth to one-quarter full. Do not compact them or press them down. Cover with warm water so the goblet is approximately two-thirds full. Process the paper until it is completely broken down. If you hear the liquidizer motor straining, switch it off and reload, as some paper has probably stuck on the blades.

To test whether the paper has completely broken down, put a tablespoon of ground-up pulp from the liquidizer goblet into a jam jar of water. Stir it thoroughly and then hold the jam jar up to the light. If you can see small pieces of paper floating in it, return it to the blender and process again. The pulp is ready when there are no paper pieces remaining in the liquid.

If you do not possess a liquidizer, you will have to soak the paper as before. Then, using a potato masher, pound it up and down in the wet paper. After you have broken the paper up roughly with

▶ *Place pieces of soaked paper into a liquidizer goblet so that it is approximately one-eighth to one-quarter full.*

▶▶ *Test the pulp by mixing some in a jam jar of water. It is ready when the water is cloudy and there are no pieces of paper floating in the water.*

the potato masher, use a kitchen mixer to mix the paper for approximately ten minutes. You will probably not achieve a completely broken-down pulp (especially if you are using a potato masher alone), but you will still be able to achieve a pleasing result.

After preparing the pulp, fill your vat to a depth of approximately 10cm (4in) with hand-hot water. Add the pulped paper. Initially you will probably need two to three liquidizer loads. You are aiming for a broth-like consistency; at the thickest it should feel like thin custard and definitely not thick porridge! If you have added too much pulp, scoop it out with a sieve, and add later as required.

Put down one of your boards next to the vat in a landscape position, and form a cross from folded newspaper on top of it. Fold another sheet to a narrower width and place it front to back on top of the cross. Place three damp felts on top of this. Prepare and have close to hand a bucket of warm water in which to dampen and squeeze out the viscose cloths. You are now ready to make your first sheet.

FORMING THE SHEET

Agitate the water in the vat and mix the pulp thoroughly with your hands to ensure that all fibres are evenly distributed through the water. Place the deckle (the open frame) on the mould (the netted frame), with the netted surface sandwiched in the middle. Hold the mould and deckle together firmly at their sides.

Slide the mould and deckle into the water, and down to the bottom of the vat. Then slide them back along the bottom of the vat and upwards out of the water keeping them level. (There is a suction as you bring the mould and deckle out of the water.) Immediately, while there is water on the mould, shake it forwards and backwards and from side to side. Forming a sheet is more effective when it is done with clear unhesitating

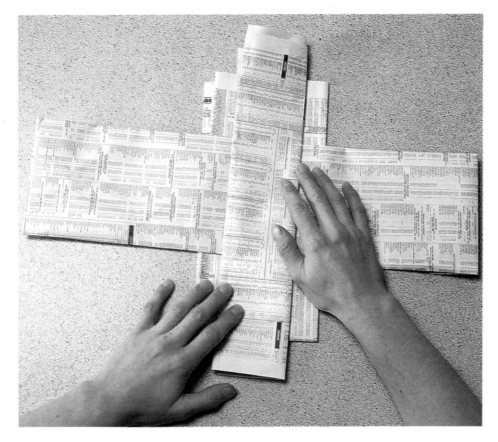

movements; try to perform the dipping in of the mould and deckle and the shaking as if they were one action.

Stop shaking the mould and deckle before the water has drained away completely. You only have a couple of seconds to do the shaking; its purpose is to bind the fibres that form the sheet together and thus make a stronger sheet. If you do not shake the mould and deckle, you will probably have sheets of even thickness straight away, but do not let a few uneven sheets at the start put you off; it will not take long to get the hang of it. Rest the mould and deckle on the side of the vat.

Take a viscose cloth and wet it in a bucket of warm water. Squeeze it out as hard as you can, so that it is just damp. Open it up, shake it to get rid of any creases and place it onto the pile of felts on the board, allowing any spare cloth to hang over the front.

▲ *To make a post, form a cross from folded newspaper. Then lay another narrower folded sheet on top, going from front to back.*

Tip the mould and deckle with one corner pointing towards the vat to encourage any excess moisture to drain from the sheet. Lift off the deckle and place it on one side, taking care not to damage the sheet. Invert the mould with the newly formed sheet onto the dampened cloth. (Do not worry, it should not fall off.) Press firmly on all of the outer edges and immediately hold the viscose cloth down with one hand and peel back the mould smoothly and quickly from the side at which you are holding the cloth.

Cover the sheet with the spare half of the viscose cloth or another dampened uncreased cloth. Should you get any creases in your cloth when you place it onto the wet sheet, lift the cloth and stretch the crease out before replacing it on the sheet as any creases will be marked in the surface of your sheet forever.

To make a new sheet, you will need a new damp felt and dampened cloth to be placed on top of the last covered sheet. More pulp will need to be added every sheet or so, depending on sheet thickness and size. The warm water from the vat can be used to mix up new pulp in the liquidizer. Keep topping the vat up with hot water as necessary, depending on the warmth and depth of the water.

If you have made a sheet that you have over-shaken, or do not like for some reason, remove the deckle and invert the mould with the sheet, so that it touches the surface of the water. The sheet will then come off. Similarly, if you make a mistake while couching (putting your newly made sheet onto the cloths), simply pick the cloth up and touch it onto the surface of the water and the sheet will come off. In both instances you will need to agitate the pulp/water

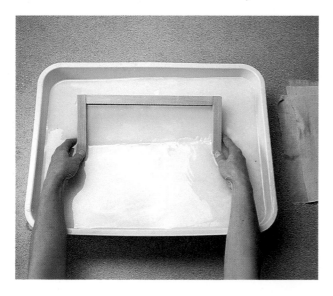

▲ *To make a sheet, agitate the vat of pulp then slide the mould and deckle into the water and down to the bottom of the vat.*

▶ *In one continuous movement, slide the mould and deckle upwards out of the water, keeping them level. Shake the mould forwards and backwards and from side to side.*

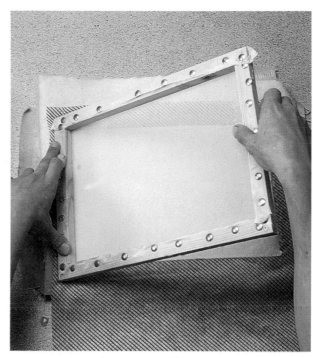

◀◀ *After the water has drained away, lift the deckle off the mould and invert the mould onto a dampened cloth.*

◀ *Press firmly on all outer edges of the mould and then peel back the mould smoothly and quickly.*

▼ *If you make a mistake when forming a sheet, remove the deckle and invert the mould into the vat. The sheet will then come off.*

mix extra well before proceeding to make the next sheet.

When you have made enough sheets of paper, or run out of viscose cloths, and can continue no further, place a final felt on top of the last viscose cloth-covered sheet and put your second board on top of that.

After finishing papermaking, wash your equipment thoroughly, in particular removing any fibres that are on the mould. A nail brush and running water are helpful, but inevitably some fibres will be stuck underneath the net or wire on the wood of the mould. Do not worry about these but, if possible, remove them at the edge, so that they do not prevent drainage through the mesh. Leave cloths and felts where they will dry properly, and if you have been using a plant, or other dye that has stained the cloths, wash these well before drying and storing them – if necessary using a mild bleach solution before washing. Dry the excess moisture from your mould and deckle and store them underneath a weighted board to prevent them warping.

STORING UNUSED PULP

Pulp, when left standing for a couple of days in warm conditions, will soon become slimy and smelly. You may find that you wish to store excess pulp for later use. Drain off the excess water through a sieve. The remaining pulp will keep for a couple of days in a refrigerator, but if you need to store it for longer you will need to freeze or dry it. Dry the pulp by hanging it in a muslin or net bag in a warm place – if you are contemplating storing pulp that contains plants or a non-dye-fast fibre, be aware that its colour may fade from its original shade, possibly at the expense of dyeing the surrounding pulp.

► *An effective way of pressing sheets is to place a pile of them on the floor, sandwiched between two boards, and then stand on them.*

► *If you have an old metal press, place the pile of sheets in the press and screw the press down tightly.*

►► *When couching a sheet, lift the viscose cloth that the sheet is laid on, onto a board with a single felt. Let the cloth and sheet sag in the centre.*

PRESSING THE SHEETS

The surface texture of your sheet will depend largely upon the method of drying and pressing that you select. Conventionally sheets are pressed, air dried and then re-pressed using many tons of pressure. But there are ways around this. For all of the following methods (except drying on a weighted cloth, when no pressing is necessary), you will first need to press the excess moisture from your sheets. You may expect, subject to the number and size of sheets made, to produce a river of water; for this operation, the garden or garage may be best suited. In all cases, continue to apply pressure until the water from the pile of papers has slowed to a drip. The drier that you can get your papers, the easier they will be to handle, as very wet sheets tend to stretch or tear when held unsupported.

Standing Place the pile of papers in their sandwiching boards on the floor and stand on it – squeeze a friend on with you if any are available!

Old press You may be fortunate enough to have access to an old metal press. Screw the press down onto the pile of papers as tightly as possible.

Car jack press If you do not have a press, a car jack is the next best thing, and is especially worth considering if you are making a larger batch of paper when drying space may be short. Place your

papers under one of the jacking points – the end with the engine is best as it is heaviest. Position the jack between the jacking point and the centre of the top board. Jack up until the vehicle is just off the ground – nothing is to be gained by going any higher.

If you intend to dry your sheet on a window or other smooth surface, I would leave it at one pressing, but if you find that your sheets are too wet to handle safely, you may either (a) repeat the above procedure, having first formed a new interleafing of sheets in their viscose cloths with any spare dry felts or newpapers that you may have, or (b) add an extra stage to the making of future sheets that will probably mean that you only need one pressing. Couch your sheet as usual, but do not leave the board at the bottom of the pile (you will still need the newspaper camber under the felts). Instead, place the board with one felt on it next to the couching area. Each time that you couch a sheet, lift the viscose cloth that the sheet is on, onto the board with the single felt. Allow the cloth and the sheet to sag at the centre as you carry it. You must try to align the sheets as accurately as possible, otherwise the sheets will receive uneven pressure, which may result in an uneven layer.

When the pile is as large as you want it to be, put on a top felt, then board and press it as usual. This method is also very useful if you have access to a spin dryer or a mangle and have only a limited supply of felts, enabling you to make more sheets for pressing in one go than you would otherwise.

If you are going to be making several different shapes or sizes of paper at one go, it will be worth separating each shape or size on a different felt-covered board. In that way a multi-storey sand-wich of boards and papers can be pressed at the same time, so giving all of the sheets of paper an even pressure.

DRYING

The method of drying you decide upon will also help determine the look of the finished paper.
Conventional air drying and re-pressing This results in a potentially smooth sheet on both surfaces, but it is dependent for a smooth finish on prolonged exposure to a lot of pressure. By using a car jack for pressure, you should be able to write on the dry sheet, but if you are only using a book for pressure, your finished sheet will have a textured surface.

Unpack the pile of papers until you come to the first sheet in its viscose cloth. Open the cloth up. Invert it onto a clean dry surface where it is to dry

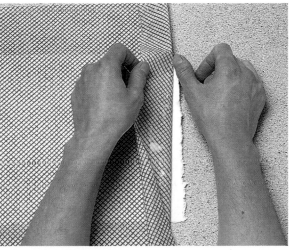

◄ *To remove the viscose cloth, peel it back until an edge of the sheet is visible. Brush downwards on the edge of the sheet with your thumb.*

◄ *The sheet will start to come off the cloth. Hold down the loosened sheet and peel back the cloth with your other hand.*

and peel back the edge of the cloth until an edge of the sheet, preferably a narrow one, is visible. Brush downwards on the edge of your sheet with a finger or thumb, and the sheet should start to come off the cloth. Hold down the loosened sheet and peel back the cloth with your other hand. As the sheets dry, they will curl up at the edges; do not put them anywhere too hot, as the faster they dry, the more they will curl and the harder they will be to flatten later.

When dry, either interleave the dry sheets between magazines and place them between boards under the jacked-up car and leave over-night, or place them between the pages of a heavy book and leave them for as long as possible and/or until you need to use them. (If using a book to press, make especially sure that the sheets are bone dry before inserting them.)

On a weighted cloth This is suitable if you are not making lots of sheets, and if drying over a couple of days or longer will not be a problem. Simply make the sheet, invert it onto a damp cloth and remove both sheet and cloth to the

▼ *As sheets dry they curl up a little at the edges. If they dry too quickly they will curl up more and it will be harder to flatten them later.*

▲ *To keep a sheet flat while it is drying, invert the sheet onto a damp cloth, then peg the cloth to the edges of a board and leave to dry.*

drying location. Bricks can be used to weight down the edges of a sheet or, by drying on a board, you can peg the cloth to the board edges. Drying in a closed cloth will result in two cloth-like surfaces or opening up a cloth (which will speed drying slightly) will result in one cloth-like and one rough surface. When the sheet is properly dry, peel it off and it is ready for use. Pressing out excess water before drying would result in a more compact sheet and speedier drying.

Ironing Unpack the pile of papers until you come to the cloth-covered sheet, and peel the sheet off. Ironing directly onto the surface of the paper will result in a polished effect, and you may prefer to iron it dry between a tea-towel, or a piece of tissue, cartridge or blotting paper.

Do not iron directly onto a piece of paper containing petals or other fragile plant frag-ments, as the heat of the iron may destroy their colour and damage them.

Drying under pressure This is a labour-intensive method of drying, but it gives the

sheet a slightly grainy but flat finish on both sides. Unpack the pile of papers and felts, leaving the sheets in their viscose cloths. Form a new interleaving of dry felts/blotting paper and sheets between two, preferably dry, outer boards. Leave under pressure (the jacked-up car, the old press or a large pile of bricks, etc). Change felts at approximately two-hourly intervals until real wetness has gone and then every 12 hours or so until completely dry. Depending upon how wet the sheets were to start with, it should take approximately six to seven changes for them to dry, but do not take them out and unpeel them from their cloth until they are quite dry as they will curl even if only slightly damp.

On a windowpane The side that is to be dried in contact with the glass is going to be very smooth. It is easiest to keep the sheet supported on the cloth as described below, which will result in the wire side (under-surface when you make it) being smooth. If you wish the felt side (uppermost surface when you make it) to be smooth, you will need first to take it off the cloth and then carefully stick it to the glass. Unpack the sheets and open up the viscose cloth. Wipe the window with a wet cloth so that the window becomes wet.

Lift the cloth with the wet sheet on it to the windowpane. Through the cloth, press the sheet onto the glass, using a pad of some sort for even pressure (for example, a screwed-up cloth), and brush from the centre outwards. When you are sure that the sheet is sticking, let it go, and peel off the cloth. You may at this stage roll it very carefully with a rolling pin so that the sheet is pressed to the glass as firmly as possible. Leave it for a few days until you are sure that it is completely dry and then carefully peel the sheet off the glass.

Paper will 'take' any surface that it dries against, so the same method may be used on wood to give a wooden grain finish. Experiment with other surfaces; there are many effects available.

NB: Newly-made sheets, especially those made by conventional air drying and re-pressing, may be prone to slight upward curling of the edges. To remedy this, after they are dry, place the sheets in a pile, and do not leave them anywhere too dry, too damp or too hot. Flip through your pile each day or so, re-arrange their order and they will soon settle down. Conventionally, sheets are left for three months to stabilize before being considered to be saleable.

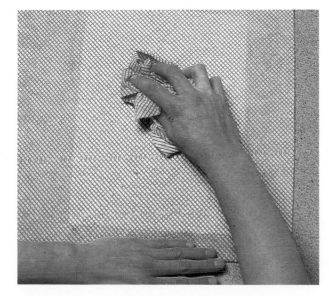

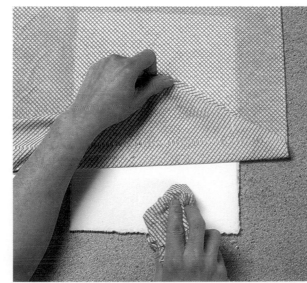

◀◀ *To dry a sheet on glass, wet the glass then place the cloth with the wet sheet on it on the glass. Press the sheet to the glass through the cloth.*

◀ *When you are sure that the sheet is sticking to the glass, let it go and peel off the cloth.*

Laminating To stick two or more wet sheets together, make a sheet as usual and put it out onto the viscose cloth. Make a second sheet and put it directly onto the first. Repeat as desired. Cover, press and dry as usual.

To sandwich objects between sheets, make a sheet as usual and lay desired objects (preferably flattish) onto the surface of the laid-down sheet. Make a second sheet and lay it directly onto the first. Cover, press and dry as usual. You may care to do this with very thin sheets (possibly without a deckle), thus making the encapsulated pieces visible when the sheet is held up to the light.

In both instances you will need to be careful of air bubbles forming in the sheets as the cloths and felts that you are working on become saturated with water. To reduce the risk, ensure that the sheets have dripped off as much excess moisture as possible before pressing onto the cloth, and lift the viscose cloth with the first sheet to one side for a moment, allowing the sheet to bend slightly in the centre while carrying. Place another damp felt on top of the pile, replace the sheet and add extra lamination. Repeat this procedure for each additional layer.

Laying items on the mould Anything that may be laid on the mould surface while the sheet is formed will have two effects: the first is that of preventing pulp settling where the obstruction is, and the second is that of leaving a deckled edge at the edge of the obstruction. Ideally the items will have enough self-weight to stay in place while you make the sheet. If not, you will have to hold or weight the item in place (small kitchen weights are very useful for this). Remove the items before couching the sheet.

If the item and the space that it leaves are more than 1–2cm ($\frac{1}{2}$–$\frac{3}{4}$in) wide, you may find that you need to simulate the effect of the mould pressing along the inner edge of the resulting hole with your finger. You may also have to take extra care while removing the sheet from the viscose cloth

▲ *To sandwich objects between sheets, lay flattish objects onto a newly formed sheet. Lay a second sheet directly on top.*

◀ *To add a coloured pattern to a sheet, make the first sheet as usual. Then pour a second coloured sheet in a swirly pattern and lay it directly onto the first.*

and brush off extra 'edges' as they are revealed in the sheet.

DECKLED EDGE

The wavy irregular edge that you get on a piece of handmade paper formed in one sheet is, I think, an intrinsic part of the feel. You may wish at some stage to control the edge by accentuating or reducing its raggedness, or even to imitate it.

Using a deckle From the point of view of removing sheets from the cloths, the edge produced by a tightly fitting deckle allowing no seepage underneath is the easiest edge to have, as it presents a fairly uniform edge for handling on a thin to medium-weight sheet. A slightly uneven deckle or mould may result in pulp seeping underneath, and a consequently ragged edge in that place. To remedy this, cut a piece of felt the same size as your deckle, and glue it to the underside of the deckle using a waterproof glue.

Using no deckle Strictly speaking, using no deckle is technically incorrect as there will be no water retained to swish and bind the fibres together, resulting in sheets that are less strong than their cousins properly shaken on a mould with a deckle. However, the irregularity of the edges of sheets made this way adds to the handmade touch, and the tissue flimsiness of these sheets seems to impart an added preciousness and even a touch of antiquity.

Set up a thin vat and simply make the sheet as usual but minus the deckle – no shaking is necessary, just bring the mould out of the water on a flat plane and keep it flat while the water runs off. Drain off excess moisture by tilting one corner back towards the vat. Press your sheet off onto a damp cloth as before. You will need to take extra care when you come to brushing the sheet off the cloth as the edge is so thin and irregular.

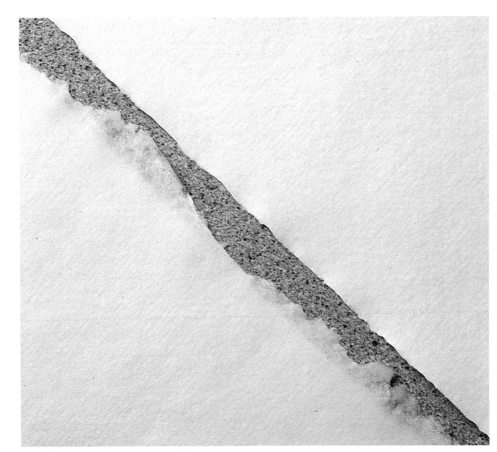

COLOURING YOUR PAPER

Colour washes of paint can obviously be applied to your paper once you have made it, but it is often useful to colour the pulp before the paper is formed. Powdered or liquid tempera colours and acrylics can be used, and even tea and coffee give soft warm tones to the paper. To ensure an even distribution of colour, the pigments should be mixed with water in the liquidizer. They should

then be added to the pulp and mixed thoroughly; remember to wipe any untinted pulp off the walls of the bucket and into the main body of colour.

If you are recycling a white or cream paper, you will find that dark intense colours can be difficult to achieve, as the paler colours of the base pulp tend to act in the same way as white, and brighten the overall effect. Using cold water dyes will result in darker colours. Follow the hand method described in the manufacturer's instructions. Before you beat up your pulp, you will need to know the dry weight of the paper that you intend to dye as one sachet only dyes 250g (8oz) of paper. Two tablespoons of washing soda can be substituted for the cold fix (it is much cheaper and has the same effect). After the dyeing time has elapsed, rinse the pulp well in a sieve under cold running water to get rid of the fixing agent.

▲ *Examples of the ragged deckled edge that you get to varying degrees on a piece of handmade paper.*

Once you have decided upon which colouring agent you are going to use, ensure that you mix more pulp than you will require if you are making a batch of papers, as it can be very difficult to get a perfect match on a subsequent mix. If you want to test the colour that you have mixed up before going any further, take a few fibres from the edge of the mix, and iron them dry through a tea-towel or something similar.

Pre-mixed colour can be squirted onto the sheet as soon as the mould is removed from the vat (you will need another pair of hands to hold the mould and deckle while you squirt the colour onto the sheet). Colour can also be squirted onto the newly formed sheet of paper before couching. This results in a more defined pattern. In both of these instances, as the paper is pressed the colours may be further mixed together, often to pleasing effect.

▼ *Colour a sheet by squirting pre-mixed colour onto the sheet as soon as the mould is removed from the vat.*

Sizing

Size is what newsprint lacks, so that if you write upon it with a water-based ink, the ink will be soaked up like blotting paper. Most commercial papers are sized and you will probably find, if you are using a recycled sized paper for your pulp, that your finished sheets retain sufficient size for you to be able to use a fine-tipped felt pen, roller ball or similar, without any noticeable spreading of the ink on the sheets.

However, in certain circumstances sizing is necessary, such as for watercolour painting, or for writing in ink across sheets incorporating plant pieces. Traditionally, sheets are sized with animal products and you may use these if you wish, but they can be smelly so I recommend using wallpaper paste and PVA glue. The very best results are achieved by stretching the paper first, as one would do to a watercolour, but this involves losing 2.5cm (1in) from each edge as the paper is cut free. For many purposes it is not, strictly speaking, necessary to stretch sheets before sizing them.

To stretch your paper Stretching should be done only to sheets of paper that are not less than three weeks old, as the older the sheets are the better the fibres have settled. Do not attempt to stretch poured or mould-dried sheets. Run cold water in a bowl large enough to be able to float your sheet in. Submerge the sheet in the water. Lift it out carefully, and place it on a flat clean sealed board or similar.

If your sheet has not gone down flat, lift and replace from the edges, gently pulling out ridges and creases. The larger the sheet that is to be stretched, the greater the care is needed, as the increasing weight of the water adds more strain on the binding fibres.

Cut some 5cm (2in) wide gummed brown or white tape into lengths approximately 10cm (4in) longer than the edges of your sheet for stretching. Wet the tape and stick it down along each edge of the paper to a depth of approximately 2.5cm (1in). As the sheet dries, it will tighten like a drum skin. When the sheet is dry, apply the size of your choice, pasting it over the surface with a paintbrush. Do not cut the paper free until the size is completely dry. In this way you can only size one surface of the sheet.

▶ *To stretch a sheet of paper, first submerge it carefully in a large bowl of cold water.*

▼ *Lift the sheet out carefully and place it on a flat, clean board. Tape down the edges with wet tape and leave to dry.*

Wallpaper paste This gives an invisible coating to the paper. If you have any plants in your paper, you will notice that, after sizing, there is a slight glazing over the petals and leaves as the size has dried on them, but you need to move the paper into the light to see this glazed effect. Lay out your sheet on a clean surface. Make up approximately 625ml (1pt) of wallpaper paste by following the instructions on the packet for sizing. Brush the thick mixture onto your paper and leave it to dry. If you wish to work on both sides of the paper, you will have to size both sides. When the first side is dry, turn the paper over, paste and leave. You should not have to apply a second coat if the paste has been well spread over the paper, but you may if you wish. Having re-wetted the sheet you may need to re-press it before proceeding, but if you like the texture that you have, this is not necessary. The wallpaper paste will keep well in an airtight jar in a refrigerator, but do not use it if it is beginning to go off.

PVA glue Using a PVA size will add a slight sheen to the whole of your paper, which will be visible when you move the paper in the light. Mix 1 part PVA with 3 parts water and proceed as for wallpaper paste.

Starch Mix together 30g (1oz) plain flour with 155ml (5fl oz) water to a paste. Heat, stirring continuously, until the mixture thickens. Apply to the sheet as for wallpaper paste.

NB: As these are all water-based techniques they will re-wet any 'unfixed' colour in your paper, for example plants which have bled colour into the paper. When the dye is re-wetted, the colour may be spread further by brushing on the size. If this is the case, you may need to spray the paper with two coats of lacquer, allowing it to dry between applications to prevent colour spreading. This, too, will add a slight sheen to the paper. Spraying sheets with lacquer is the fastest (but most expensive) option as it dries very quickly.

Projects

These projects have been chosen to use the full range of papermaking techniques. They include quick and easy projects, such as greetings cards, as well as unusual ideas for the more ambitious including a notebook and place mat. Most are fairly inexpensive to do – all they require is your time. They are, of course, initial ideas and will hopefully lead you on to create other projects of your own.

Drawer liner

Drawer liners, delicately perfumed and decorated with pretty flowers, make lovely and thoughtful presents. If you are planning to roll up a drawer liner in order to wrap it, remember not to include plant pieces in the paper that are too large as they will come away from the paper as it is rolled.

You will need:
- Sheets of handmade paper, possibly made with pretty or fragrant flowers or seed heads, for example lavender heads
- Spray-on shoe protector
- Essential oil
- Ribbons (optional)
- Hole punch (optional)

1 *Take your chosen sheet of paper and trim it to fit the drawer, if necessary. Spray shoe protector onto the side that you intend to be facing uppermost in the drawer. Allow it to dry.*

2 *Drip a few drops of the essential oil onto the unsprayed side of the drawer liner (lavender and lemon grass are reputed to act as insect repellants but you can use your favourite mixture), and allow it to dry.*

3 *The liner is now ready to go into a drawer with the oiled side facing downwards. If you need to make larger sheets to cover a drawer completely, and do not have a sheet large enough, join two or more sheets together by threading ribbons in and out through punched holes along adjoining edges. Allow at least twice the length to be joined in ribbon. To ensure the drawer liner retains the perfume of the essential oil, add a few more drops every few months or so.*

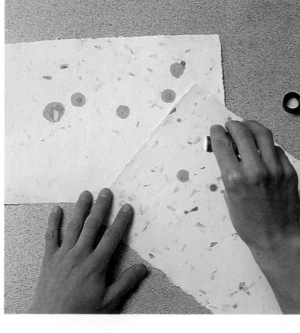

▲ *Drip a few drops of essential oil onto the side of the drawer liner that has not been sprayed with shoe protector and allow to dry. Repeat every few months to ensure the drawer liner retains the scent.*

▲ *To make a drawer liner larger than an A4 sheet, join two or more sheets together. Punch several holes along adjoining edges of the sheets, then weave ribbons in and out of the punched holes.*

Picture mount

The soft edge of these mounts offers a refreshing change from the usual straight edge of a commercially available picture mount. You can design your mount to pick up colours in the pictures that you wish to mount, or even incorporate into the paper fragments from an event or place, for example grasses and sand from your holiday around a holiday photo.

You will need:
- Cutting knife
- Plastic envelope stiffener
- Skewer
- Screw
- Vat of pulp
- Mould and deckle
- Felts
- Viscose cloths
- Boards
- Sponge

1 Select the shape and size mount that you wish to create, bearing in mind that going to within 1.5cm ($\frac{5}{8}$in) or less of the sheet edge is not advisable. Cut out the shape that you require the aperture to be from plastic envelope stiffener or thick tape-covered cardboard. Pierce the centre of your shape with a skewer, and thread the screw through the hole.

2 Set up your papermaking equipment. Place the shape that you have made into the position on the mould where you want the final aperture to be. Hold your mould and deckle firmly, with your thumbs resting on the aperture shape to prevent it floating away in the water, and make the sheet as usual.

3 After removing the deckle, dab the shape with a sponge to remove excess water, then carefully lift the shape up, holding onto the screw.

4 When couching, in addition to pressing on your deckle, you must simulate the effect of a deckle by pressing down with your finger next to the inner edge, and then remove the mould as usual. Dry and press as wished.

VARIATIONS
Multiple apertures *To make a mount with more than one aperture, you will require help to hold the shapes in place – or kitchen scale weights would do the job.*
Double mount *To give a professional finish, either make two mounts in contrasting colours in the same shape but of slightly different aperture size, or buy the mount with the smaller aperture and make the top mount to contrast. The minimum difference in size should be 1–1.5cm ($\frac{1}{2}$–$\frac{5}{8}$in) to allow for the deckle edge.*

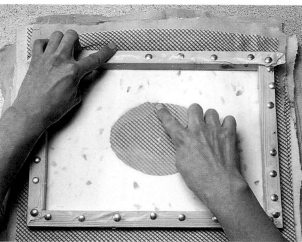

▲▲ *Sponge off any excess water from the aperture shape, then carefully lift it up, holding it by the screw in its centre.*

▲ *When couching the sheet, press down with your finger next to the inner edge to simulate the effect of a deckle.*

Panels of paper

Notelets and especially cards are a simple way of using even your most textured, holey or creased sheets of paper. Alternatively, if you have just a little of a paper you really like, this could help eke it out. The method also avoids the conflicts of finding suitable envelopes provided that you can find a mounting card and envelope that match.

You will need:
- Handmade paper
- Scalpel
- Metal-edged ruler
- Mounting card
- Adhesive
- Powdered gold and silver tempera colours or ink
- Paper adhesive
- PVA glue
- Paintbrush
- Plant material (optional)

Cut panels

Cut your sheet of paper into panels, taking care to cut the edges parallel. Leaving one deckled edge in place can be effective. Mount the paper onto the front of the chosen card using paper adhesive.

Deckled panels

Make special panels with four deckled edges. Make up a special mould and deckle, or use a special deckle on your larger mould, or put in dividers to your ordinary deckle to make several panels at once.

As an inner leaf

You can purchase or even make window cards. They usually consist of three panels of similar width, folded to conceal the back of the inlaid sheet. All that you need do is to glue your chosen sheet of paper in position.

Collages

These provide the ideal opportunity to use up your disasters; tear or cut them up and reform them into 'landscapes', weavings, geometric or asymmetric designs.

Colouring the edges of your panels

Mix a heaped teaspoonful of gold or silver powdered tempera colour with a teaspoon of water, add a tiny dab of PVA, and mix well. Brush the mix onto the edge of your paper, and leave to dry before gluing to the final card.

Placing plants on the panels

To achieve an exact arrangement of plants, you can laminate two thin layers with your 'sandwich' of plants in the middle – this will result in a subtle effect. For a bolder effect lay the plants that you wish to use in position, and then carefully pour small handfuls of pulp over parts of the plant to bond it into place.

Some of the plant pieces may become detached as they air dry. Press drying will significantly increase the success rate, as will using pre-pressed flowers.

▲ *Colour the edge of a panel with gold or silver tempera colour mixed with PVA and leave to dry.*

▶ *Place leaves on a sheet and pour small handfuls of pulp over parts of the leaves to bond them to the paper.*

Randomly dyed cards

Children tend to be expert at this technique as they love squirting the paint and, in this instance, the more paint the better the results.

You will need:
- Soft plastic bottles with lids or squirting mechanisms
- Skewer
- Assortment of paint colours, one for each bottle
- Vat of pulp
- Mould and deckle
- Felts
- Viscose cloths
- Boards

1 Make two or three holes in the top of the bottles with a skewer. Push through from the outside to the inside. Do not make the holes too large, but if you find that they are so, you can partially blank them with tape. Put various paint colours in the bottles and add water so that the colours are still strong but not too thick, as they must be able to be squirted easily.

2 Make sheets as usual and either squirt in paint with the aid of another pair of hands as the sheet is removed from the vat and shaken, and/or when the sheet has drained. If you wish to keep the vat the original colour, you must squirt the paint and shake the mould away from the vat so that no colour drains through into the water. Do not skimp on the paint as you need enough to go through the viscose cloth and colour the adjacent sheets as well. Several colours can be applied simultaneously.

3 Couch the sheet as usual. Remove the sheets to a separate pile (see page 21) so that a much thinner than usual post of papers is made. Press them as hard as you can.

4 Remove the sheets from the cloths and dry. The paints will need washing out of the cloths and felts immediately to prevent them staining an adjacent sheet later. For this reason you may also care not to press dry the sheets, as you will cover so many felts with paint.

Child's hand-painted card
While making a sheet, place a child's outspread hand onto the mould. The hand should remain in place until the sheet has drained. The result is a three-dimensional shadow of the hand, best seen against the light or a darker coloured card. For an invitation, mount the sheet onto a card of contrasting colour or use a paper liner.

Greetings card messages
You can purchase sheets of standard greetings transfers to use inside or on the cover of your card. These are available in gold and silver as well as black, and they include numbers so that you can make up your own message.

▶ *Squirt paint onto a sheet as it is being removed from the vat and shaken.*

▶ *Make a sheet with a child's outspread hand in position on the mould. Keep the hand in place until the sheet has drained.*

Notebook

In this project all the papers in the book are handmade. You could of course reduce the number of sheets used by substituting suitable commercial papers, or by reducing the number of pages in the book. You can also use the same technique to make a larger book.

You will need:

- 14 pieces of A5 matching paper
- Wooden board
- Scalpel
- Metal-edged ruler
- Needle
- Cotton thread
- Candle
- Scissors
- Bias binding facing material
- Two A5 neutral or contrasting sheets, for the end papers
- PVA glue
- Stiff card/mounting board
- Iron-on material, eg buckram, for the spine
- Brush
- Pen

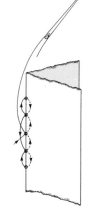

THE INSIDE OF THE BOOK

1 Take 12 of the matching A5 sheets and divide them into three groups of four. Face all of the sheets right-side up, and fold them in half widthways.

2 Place one of the sets of four sheets right-side up on the wooden board. Pierce five small holes through the layers with a scalpel, along the centre fold at 2.5, 5, 7.5, 10 and 12.5cm (1, 2, 3, 4 and 5in) from one of the outer edges. Repeat this for the two other groups, always using the same side to measure the hole spacing.

3 Thread a needle with double cotton that has been run along a wax candle a few times (this lends extra strength to the cotton). Taking one of the pierced sets, sew into the central hole from the side that will become the spine. Weave the needle and thread in and out as shown, so that the last cotton comes out of the same hole as the first. Avoid putting the needle through the ready-threaded cotton, to prevent it from tangling. Tie a double knot around the long central thread. Cut off ties at 12mm ($\frac{1}{2}$in) lengths. Repeat for the remaining two sections except for the last section, when you should proceed as before, but do not cut off the cotton thread.

4 Use the remaining cotton to thread a weave in between the cotton ties, weaving the length of the spine and back. When complete, tie off with a double knot and cut off the thread with 12mm ($\frac{1}{2}$in) ties remaining.

5 Cut a 14cm (5$\frac{1}{2}$in) length of the self-adhesive interfacing material, and iron it on around the spine as tightly as possible. Alternatively, you could use three or four material tapes, 12mm ($\frac{1}{2}$in) wide, glued around the spine to extend 2cm ($\frac{3}{4}$in) on the pages of the book.

▲▲ *Using a scalpel, pierce five small holes through the layers of the sheets at 2.5cm (1in) intervals.*

▲ *Using a needle and double cotton, sew the layers together, weaving the needle in and out of the holes.*

6 Fold the two plain sheets in half widthways. Place a piece of waste paper inside the first page to extend over the edges. Paste PVA glue onto the outside of the first page, right up to the edges and, lining it up carefully, stick on one of the plain sheets. Repeat for the back page and the last remaining sheet. Remove the protective sheets from the inside after removing any excess glue, and place them under a weight to dry.

THE COVER

1 Protect the cover sheets by spraying on a coat of shoe protector and leaving it to dry.

2 Cut the two boards to about 15.5 × 11.5cm (6¼ × 4½in). This measurement depends on how ragged your deckled edges are; the boards should overlap the edges by 3mm (⅛in) on three opening sides.

3 Remove the inside of the book from its weighted position and press between the newly cut boards to check that they fit. If correct, measure the width from one outer edge to the other. Cut a spine for the book as long as the boards and as wide as the total measured width.

4 Cut the material for the spine to approximately 9 × 19cm (3½ × 7½in). (You need an overlap of approximately 2–2.5cm (¾–1in) at the top and bottom of the book.) Test a small patch of the material to find if the PVA glue goes through to the front side. If it does, spray with shoe protector and move it to another position to dry. When it is dry, mark the centre line with a pen. Brush on the PVA glue. Place the centre of the 'spine' board along the central line, allow a 3mm (⅛in) gap and place on the cover boards to the right and the left. Check the measurements before pressing them down firmly. All three of the boards must be in alignment at the top and bottom. Fold over the excess material into the inside at both ends.

5 Take one of the two remaining pieces of paper and place them face-down. Position one board in the required position over the paper, overlapping the paper onto the spine to the preferred width. Fold over the upper and lower edges. Trim the remaining edge to a width of 2.5cm (1in). Cut across at the corners at 45°, 2.5cm (½in) from the corner and fold.

◄ Paste PVA glue onto the outside of the first page, right up to the edges, and stick it on one of the plain sheets.

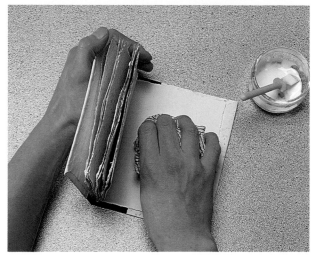

◄ Insert the centre sections of the notebook, applying extra PVA glue as necessary and pressing with a cloth to smooth out any air bubbles.

6 Cover the inside of the paper up to the edges with PVA glue. Place the sheet on a clean surface and put the book back into position. Fold the upper and lower edges and then the outer edge, applying extra PVA as necessary to the doubled folds. Smooth out any air bubbles and press firmly. Repeat for the other cover paper.

7 Place a protective sheet under the fly leaf page at one end and cover the outside page to its edges with PVA glue. Remove the protective sheet and stick it into position carefully on the front inner board, working from the spine outwards. Repeat for the back cover, and brush PVA onto the spine before stitching the cover down. Remove any excess glue then leave it under a weighted board to dry.

Place mat

Paper is a very good insulating material, and is therefore ideal for making table mats. This project uses the technique of laminating, so that you have two layers of paper sandwiching a layer of pansies in between.

You will need:
- Dark-coloured pansies or other alternative
- Vat of pulp
- Mould and deckle
- Felts
- Viscose cloths
- Boards
- Pair of tweezers
- Rubber gloves
- Cotton wool ball
- Cellulose dope or polyurethane varnish and brush
- Hard board (optional)
- PVA glue (optional)
- Undercoat and gloss paint (optional)
- Felt (optional)

To achieve a good protective layer, you will have to set up your vat with so much pulp that it feels like porridge. To do the laminating thinly enough, so that you can see the encaptured pansies, you will need a second vat, set up with very little pulp. Alternatively, you could make the thick sheets and spread them out on their cloths, readjust your vat and then add the second sheet to the first, on the top of a fresh felt. To prevent the flowers from 'melting' too quickly, and becoming difficult to handle, make these sheets in a cool air temperature and a cool vat.

1 Pick blue and/or black pansies when they are dry. (Blue pansies are best, and look good combined with some black ones. If you have to pick them when it is wet, be sure that they are dry before putting them into the freezer.) Spread the flowers and stems onto a baking tray or similar. Do not overlap the plants. Put them into the freezer. Ensure that the plants are completely frozen before working with them, or the effect will not be so good.

2 Make a thick sheet using a deckle to retain the maximum possible amount of pulp. Couch it onto a cloth as usual.

3 Take the tray of pansies from the freezer. Pick up each pansy with a pair of tweezers and position it on your sheet. Continue until you have an arrangement that pleases you — bear in mind that what you see will diffuse somewhat as it dries. Return the pansies to the freezer as soon as you have taken what you need. If you have to rearrange the pansies, use the tweezers — the heat from your hand could melt the petals.

4 When you have an arrangement that you like, make a second very thin sheet without the deckle. Make a few small holes in the sheet while still on the mould where the pansies will be, so that a part of the petal will be exposed, and the veining will be visible in the finished sheet. Ensure that the pansies have 'melted' before pressing the second sheet into position. If the pansies still seem to be frozen, breathe on them for a few seconds.

5 Repeat the procedure for each mat, putting two felts between each sheet to ensure that no dye from one sheet will inadvertently stain another. When finished, put the board on top of the final felt, and press.

▲ *Using tweezers to handle the frozen pansies, to avoid melting the petals,* *arrange them individually on the sheet until you have a design you like.*

6 Use the 'press dry' method for drying, using two dry felts between each sheet in its cloth. Every time you change the felts, peel back the viscose cloth on the top side and have a look at the paper. The dye will keep spreading. When you have an effect that you like, increase the frequency of felt changing to, say, once an hour, so that the effect will not spread any further. When the sheet is 100 per cent dry, remove it from the cloth. You will have to wash both the felts and the cloths that have been stained in a mild bleach solution to remove the dye that will reactivate when it is wet, as it may otherwise stain any later sheets that it comes into contact with.

7 To protect your finished mats, using rubber gloves and a cotton wool ball, rub cellulose dope into the surface. Give one good coat to each side, allowing them to dry before turning them to the second side. Take great care when doing the deckled edges. Then press under a large book, if necessary, when dry. If cellulose dope is not available, polyurethane gloss or matt varnish may be painted on, but it does not give the virtually invisible finish of the cellulose dope.

8 Alternatively, cut a piece of hardboard approximately 5cm (2in) larger in each direction than your sheet. Paint the sides and the edges that will be exposed with size, undercoat and gloss paint of your chosen coordinated colour, allowing each coat to dry before applying the next. Apply cellulose dope or polyurethane varnish to the front of the paper as above. When dry, fix into place, using a non-water-based glue and being very careful to ensure that the deckled edges are firmly stuck. If you have used polyurethane varnish, you can give a final coat to the top of the finished mat to help the deckled edges to stick. Cover the back of the board with felt and glue in position. Alternatively, you can take your chosen sheets to a printer for lamination between two layers of plastic for an effect similar to an ID card.

VARIATIONS
Different flowers may be used; experiment, but as a rule of thumb, you will find that the darker the petals, the more intense is the colour that is yielded. Different-coloured pulps can be used, but they will tint each other, for example reds will change whites to pinks. If you are using two colours, place the darker colour down first, even if this means placing the flowers on backwards.
To make matching napkin rings, set up dividers in your deckle to make strips of paper. Laminate as for the place mat, then punch or pierce each strip into a loop fastened with an appropriate thread or ribbon, and coat it in a layer of cellulose dope.

▶ *The finished place mats.*

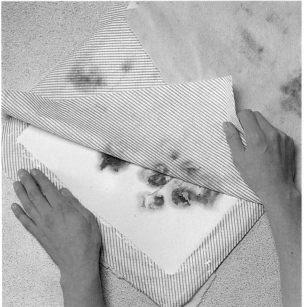

◀◀ *As the paper dries, the dye will spread. Peel back the viscose cloth on the top side to check the effect on the paper.*

◀ *To protect your finished mat, rub a coat of cellulose dope into the surface using a cotton wool ball and wearing rubber gloves.*

Marbling

Marbling is an ancient craft which remained cloaked in mystery until this century. The oldest form of marbling on paper began in 12th-century Japan. Known as *suminagashi*, which literally means 'floating ink', the art was handed from one generation to the next by a custom of teaching the process to only one child in a family. For several hundred years, the use of marbled paper was restricted to the royal household only.

The earliest documented sheet of marbled paper, known as Ebru, dates from the 15th century and came from the Near East. It was here that glue was first added to water to form size. This gave marblers much more control over their colours, and formed the basis of today's marbling techniques.

In England, marbling only became an important industry in the nineteenth century, when the first book to explain marbling techniques appeared. Published by Woolnough in 1853, it caused consternation that hitherto well-kept secrets had finally been given away. Up till then, masters had kept their secrets by never teaching the whole process to any one apprentice. In this century, the craft was kept alive virtually single-handedly in England by the binders and marblers Cockerell and Sons.

Since the 1970s, marbling has found a new popularity. It is no longer used only by bookbinders but has acquired new devotees among designers and manufacturers, who have come to appreciate the many uses marbling designs may be put to. I now regularly produce special designs for an amazing variety of uses − from borders to greeting cards to packaging for supermarket tissue boxes, and even packaging for condoms!

The fascination of transferring floating inks or paints on to paper appeals to all ages, however. There is a kind of magic in the process.

Marbling has always given me an enormous amount of enjoyment. I very much hope that you will have as much pleasure as I have in experimenting with different paints and patterns.

Equipment and Techniques

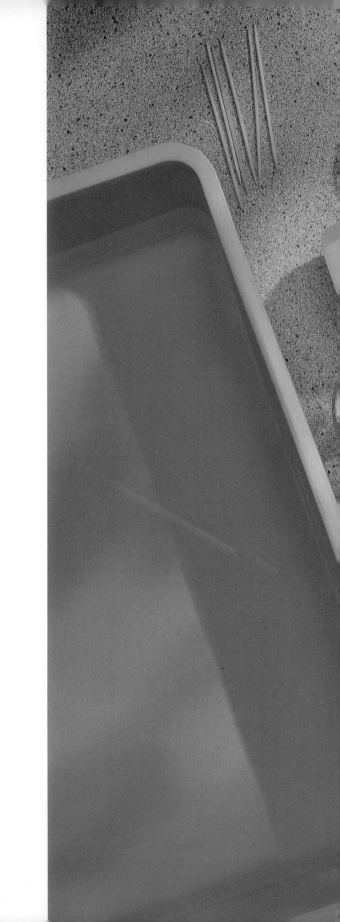

Marbling is an ideal craft for beginners because most of the equipment needed is readily available and cheap. And because there are no rigid rules, many of the items you need can be easily adapted from things around the house. All marbling techniques work from the principle of spattering paints onto size, then swirling them with a stylus to make interesting patterns, a skill you will quickly develop with practice.

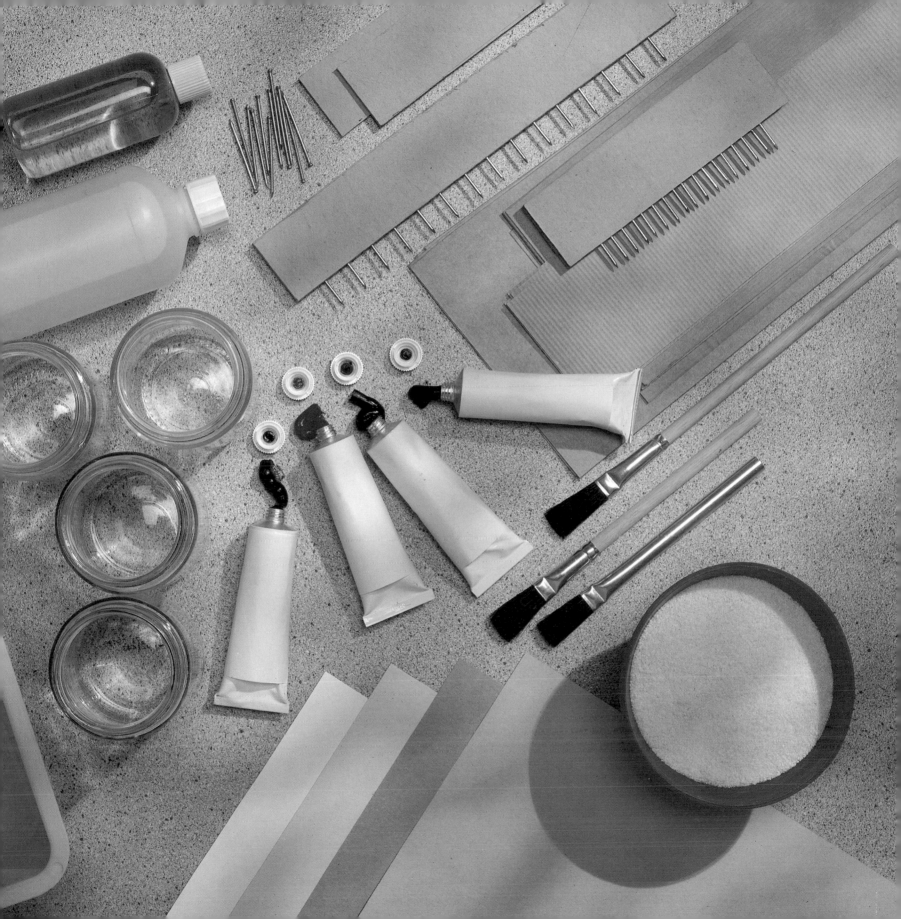

Equipment and materials

MARBLING IS A MARVELLOUS MEANS OF SELF-expression. It is also, unfortunately, rather messy, so your first important consideration will be to find somewhere to do it. You will need a table with enough space for your pots of paint and brushes – and, preferably, a large free area around it. I also always recommend sheets of plastic to protect the floor, and, if there's a wall in front of the table, a covering for that too. The paint flies everywhere!

For the best results, you will also need the right atmospheric conditions. Marbling, alas, is not synonymous with comfort and the ideal conditions are slightly damp, cool and dust-free. A garden shed is perfect! Access to fresh air is vital to avoid the fumes from the white spirit you will be using to thin the paint. If using water-based paints, you

must also have a sink or outside tap at hand for rinsing your marbled paper.

Once you have established all these requirements, you can then concentrate on more specific equipment. Below are all the basics you will need for oil and water marbling. Bear in mind that you will need additional combs as you start to experiment with more complicated patterns.

ALUM

Alum solution is sponged over all paper that is marbled with water-based paints, to make the paper absorb the paints properly. You will not need it when working with oil paints. (Don't forget: you will also need a sponge to apply the solution, and rubber gloves to protect your hands.)

Key Diagram

1 Marbling tank
2 Cocktail sticks (to use as a stylus)
3 Ox gall
4 White spirit
5 Panel pins and comb
6 Pots for mixing paints
7 Paints
8 Paintbrushes
9 Paste powder
10 Selection of papers

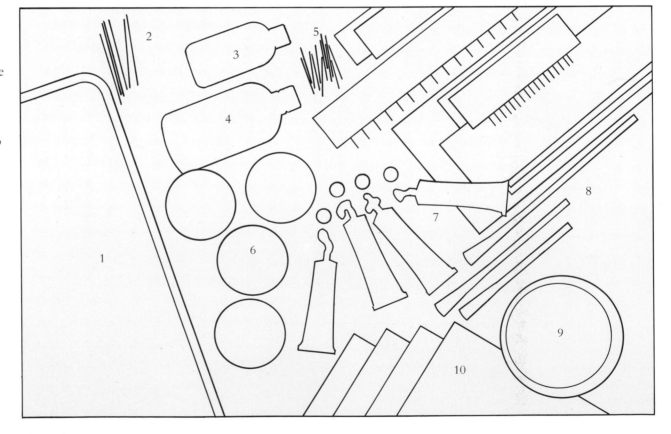

BRUSHES, EYEDROPPERS AND POTS

Brushes are generally only used with oil paints. Almost any bristle paintbrush from a hardware shop or decorating suppliers will do. Brushes are measured by the width of the bristle, and the ones most often used in marbling measure 6mm (¼in), 12mm (½in) and 2.5cm (1in), though the wider 2.5cm (1in) brush will generally only be used for applying background colour. The width and length of bristles are important if you are to control your paint properly. Children's paintbrushes, for example, are very well suited to marbling, but you may have to cut the bristles if they are too long, to stop the paint from flying about. Similarly, brushes that are too chunky will take up too much paint, which will cause problems when trying to control the amount of paint landing on the paper.

Eyedroppers are used instead of brushes when working with watercolours. They are not suitable for oil paints because they are too difficult to clean.

Pots are used for mixing the paints. Anything such as a jam jar or coffee tin will do, as long as it is wide enough to mix your paints easily. Yogurt pots are useful because they are disposable, but they are also very light, so watch out that your brush doesn't tip the pot over.

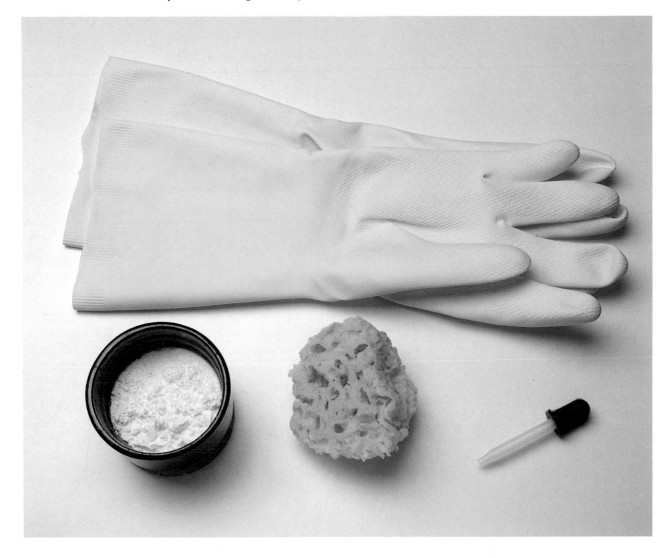

The four items illustrated here – alum, eyedropper, sponge and rubber gloves – are used only for marbling with watercolours. They are not needed at all for oil paints.

COMBS

Combs are used to create specific patterns, which will vary according to the width between the teeth in the comb. (The narrower the teeth, the more intricate the pattern.) A hair comb with long teeth – the type used for permed hair – can achieve quite effective results, but the best option is to make your own.

One simple way of doing this is to bang panel pins through a piece of thin (about 12mm (½in) thick) plywood which measures either the length or width of your marbling tank. For a first attempt, panel pins set 12mm (½in) apart will give an easy

comb to make and use. It may be easier to use if you attach a knob handle on top.

An alternative method is to stick long dressmaker's pins into a narrow piece of balsa wood – the sharp end into the wood. This is the quickest way of all to make a marbling comb, but be warned: if you use the comb a great deal, the paint will eventually build up on the pin heads and you will not be able to produce clean, flowing patterns.

A third, inexpensive, way of making a comb is described and illustrated below. Like the other two versions, it has pins set 12mm (½in) apart – the most suitable width for a beginner. As you progress

1

MAKING A COMB

Cut two pieces of cardboard about 7.5cm (3in) deep by the length you require. Attach double-sided tape to one of the pieces.

2

Distribute the pins 12mm (½in) apart and lay them on double-sided tape so that they will not move.

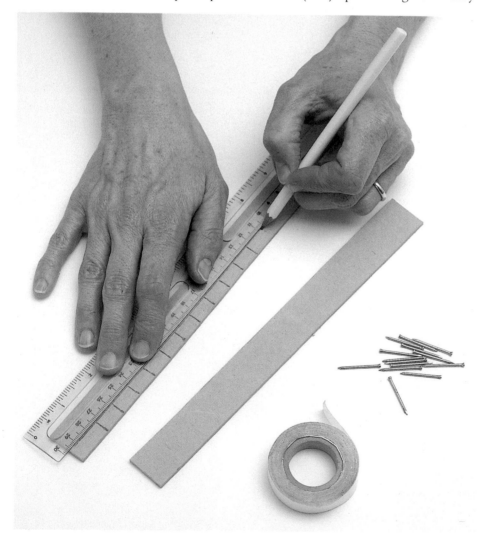

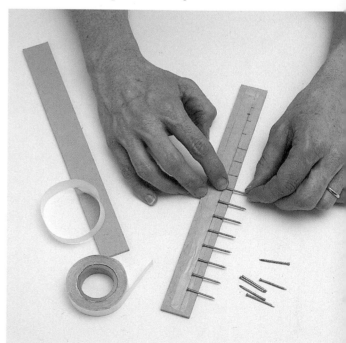

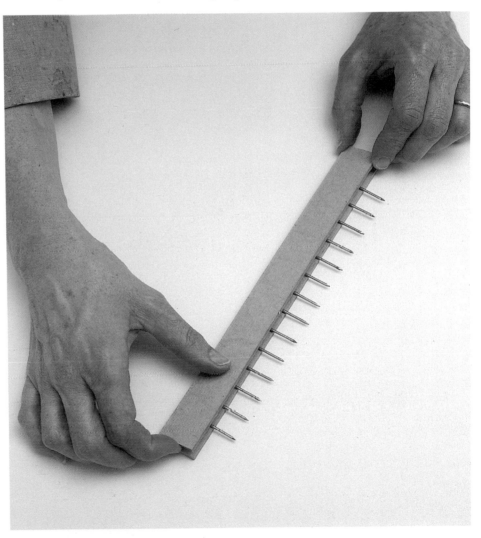

you will need two further combs – one with pins set 6mm (¼in) apart and another with pins set 3mm (⅛in) apart.

DRYING RACK

All marbled sheets need to be left to dry. A concertina clothes drying rack is perfect, or you can make up a line of string with clothes pegs and peg the paper on that. Alternatively, you could have a plastic sheet or newspaper to lay the marbled sheets on. It really depends on how much space you have and how many sheets of paper you marble at a time.

MARBLING TANK

This is where you will actually create your patterns and lay your paper on the surface of the size, so you need to bear the following factors in mind. The tank should, ideally, be flat-bottomed, and about 5cm (2in) deep. It can be slightly deeper than this, but not too much or you may find it difficult to lay the paper evenly on the surface. It should also be at least 2.5cm (1in) larger all round than the paper you want to marble, to allow enough room for your fingers to lay the paper down.

Marbling tanks can be made from a variety of materials, such as metal or watertight plastic. You

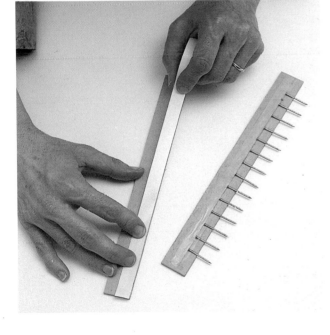

3

Lay another strip of double-sided tape on to the second piece of cardboard and press down firmly to secure.

4

Press the two pieces of cardboard firmly together to complete the final stage of the comb.

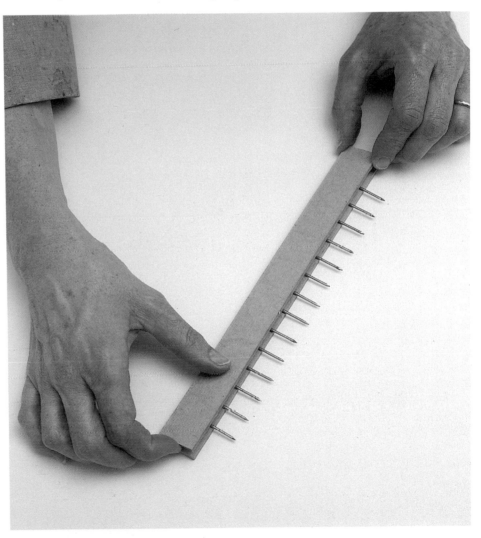

can even make your own, using heavy-duty plastic (the type used for lining ponds) nailed to strips of wood, although once you become experienced you may prefer to have one tailor-made for you by a blacksmith. If you're a beginner, however, a cat litter tray is probably the cheapest and most accessible option although once you start using large sheets of paper, you will have to progress to something bigger.

Bear in mind that your tank will need to be continually emptied, so if you do decide to have one made, it should have a draining tap at one end. A tank full of size is heavy so bear this in mind when you plan where you are going to marble. You will either need to empty the tank into a bucket or carry it to a suitable drain.

PAINTS, THINNERS AND OX GALL

Paints for marbling can be either oil- or water-based. My own particular preference is for oil paints – either artist's or student's oils, though the latter are cheaper. Whichever you choose, thin them with white spirit, not turpentine which will be too oily. Any water-based paints such as poster paints can be used, though these will, of course, be thinned with water.

Ox gall is the vital ingredient for any marbler, whichever type of paint you are using, to reduce the surface tension on the water or size, and to help the paints disperse properly on the surface of the tank. You can also try washing up liquid – it is certainly cheaper – although you may need to experiment with amounts a little at first.

Plain brown paper is perfect for experimenting with as a beginner, but as your marbling skills improve you can progress to other types of paper. Tinted papers, ranging from pale to dark colours, offer particularly interesting effects. The same paint can change dramatically when applied on to the different shades.

PAPER

The best paper to use for marbling is uncoated paper – that is, any paper which does not have a very shiny surface. If the paper is too slippery, the paints won't be absorbed. If it is too thin, it will tear when wet. A good example is tissue paper, which looks very pretty when marbled, but will disintegrate if it absorbs too much water.

Any type of fairly strong, absorbent paper is ideal. Plain brown, or kraft, paper is perfect for experimenting because it is so cheap. The same applies to copy paper, which is another cheap alternative. You can always progress to more expensive bond or laid paper later, as you become more skilled.

Tinted or textured papers can produce very interesting effects. Used with gold and silver paints, they can make attractive and unusual giftwrapping paper.

PAPER STRIPS

You will need strips of newspaper or any other absorbent paper to clean the surface of the tank after marbling each sheet. They should, ideally, measure 5–7.5cm (2–3in) wide by the length of the marbling tank you are using.

SIZE

Size is a mixture of water and gelatine, and is used to hold the pattern. It can be made from Courlose powder, or, more commonly, carragheen moss (Irish seaweed). Non-fungicide wallpaper paste, if you can find it, is also acceptable.

STYLUS

Styluses are used to create a swirl or feather pattern. They are also used in the first step of all combed patterns. The basic requirement for any stylus is that it should be fairly thin and easy to pick up. If you don't have a stylus, there are many things you can use instead, such as darning needles, cocktail sticks, or any long wire rod. My own particular preference is for thin knitting needles.

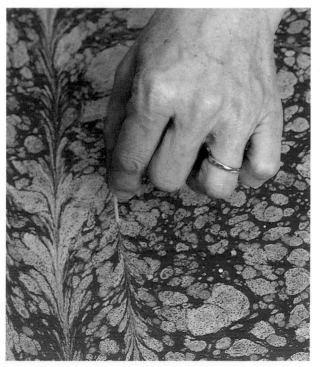

You will need paper strips to clean the surface of the tank. Any type of absorbent paper can be used – the more absorbent it is, the more quickly it will absorb any residual paint.

Anything can be used for a stylus as long as it is thin and fairly easy to pick up. Cocktail sticks can be particularly useful because they are disposable once the build-up of paint gets too heavy.

Basic techniques

THE ART OF MARBLING IS ACHIEVED BY FLOAT-ing paints on the surface of water or size (a mixture of water and gelatine) in a marbling tank. Beginners may find it easier to float the paints on water. However, using a thickened size with a stylus and different-sized combs will give you a wider variety of patterns.

Either oil- or water-based paints can be used. There's a lot to be said for starting off with water-based paints such as poster paints. They are cheaper, washable, and safe for small children. The only difference between oil- and water-based paints in terms of technique is that if you are using water-based paints you will have to sponge the paper with an alum solution first, to help the paints stick to the paper. Paper marbled with water-based paints must also be rinsed after being removed from the marbling tank. (The alum is important here, otherwise the paints will disappear along with the rinsing water!)

To make the alum solution, mix 60g (2oz) alum with 625ml (1 pint) of very hot water then stir until

It's very important to use a continuous movement when laying your paper on the surface of the size. Any hesitation at all may cause a watermark, as shown here.

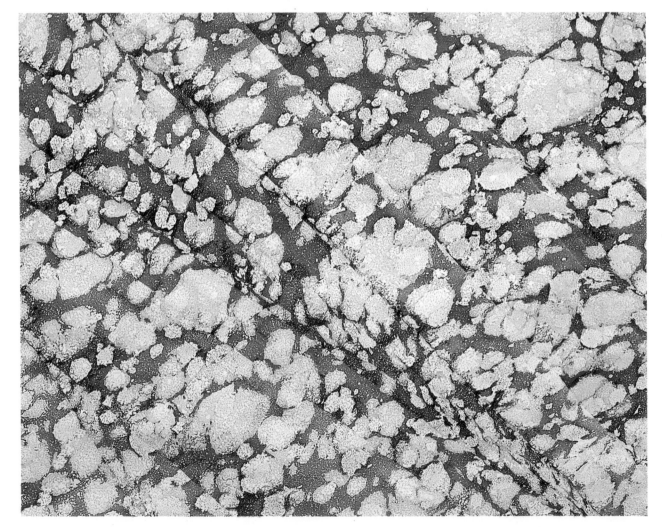

dissolved. As soon as the solution is cool enough it will be ready to use. If you decide to use water-based paints all the time, I suggest you set aside a container especially for making the solution.

Whichever paint you use, the first thing you must do is to prepare the size, or solution on which the paints are floated (see page 56).

PREPARING THE PAINTS

Once you have made the size, the next stage is to select and prepare your paints. Choose between two and four colours to begin with until you have mastered how to mix them.

Squeeze approximately 2–3cm (1–1½in) paint into each of your separate pots, adding a little white spirit to each pot to thin the paint slightly – the paints should be runny but not too thin. Then add just a few drops of ox gall and mix well into the paints. Oil paints don't take kindly to being left standing overnight, so it's best to use them as soon as you have mixed them.

DISTRIBUTING THE PAINTS

After preparing your paints you must learn how to distribute them evenly on the size (see below). The secret here is to have just the right amount of paint on the brush to make the paint fall in a fine spray. If you have too much, the paint will fall in blobs and sink below the surface of the size instead of floating on the surface. So remove as much paint as possible against the edge of the pot before beginning. It is best to practise flicking the paint with a firm but small flick of the wrist. You may find it easier at first to tap your brush against an old pencil or piece of wood to achieve the desired effect. That way you will be able to control the amount of paint on the size.

Like any other new subject, distributing the paint needs practice, so don't be discouraged if your first effort is less than perfect. As you become more skilled, you will learn to recognize problems as they arise. If the paint sinks, for example – and

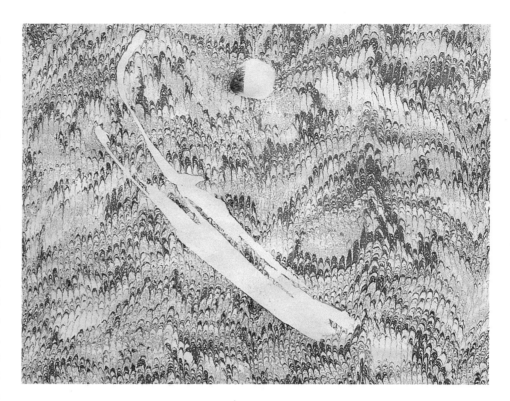

assuming this is not because you have applied too much – it is probably too thick and needs thinning with a little more white spirit. The temperature of the size is also crucial. Paints will spread better if the size is at room temperature. If the size is too cold, the paints will contract. If, on the other hand, the paints spread too much they are either too thin or will have too much ox gall, although the odd blob of paint on the surface can be dispersed by blowing it gently.

PATTERNS AND PRINTS

When you have distributed all the paints successfully on the size, you can then proceed to the real business of marbling: creating patterns by drawing a stylus or a knitting needle across the surface of the tank in a swirling motion. The final stage of the process is to make a print by laying your paper on the size, then leaving it to dry. You have now produced your first sheet of marbled paper!

The instructions on pages 56–59 are for oil marbling on cellulose size.

If, when laying paper on the surface of the size, air is trapped between the two, an air bubble, or blank patch, will appear on the paper as illustrated here. Always be sure to press the paper down carefully on the size to make sure the whole sheet makes contact with the paints.

MAKING THE SIZE

Fill the tank with cold water to a depth of 3–5cm (1½–2in). Sprinkle a few tablespoonfuls of Courlose powder on the surface, stirring continuously until dissolved. The prepared size should be the consistency of very well diluted wallpaper paste and should move slightly when a stylus is drawn across it. (If necessary, add more powder.)

1

ADDING THE PAINTS

Take a strip of paper and draw it across the surface of the size to remove any particles of dust or paint. Stir each pot of paint with a brush and remove as much paint as possible against the edge of the pot. Flick your first colour on to the surface of the size so that the paint falls evenly over the surface in a fine spray.

2

Continue adding the rest of the first colour with a flicking action. This background colour should fully cover the surface of the tank.

3

Add the rest of your colours with the same flicking action. Don't pause between colours or surface tension in the size will build up, and the paints will not spread properly.

MARBLING (swirl pattern)
When all your colours are on the tank, slowly, but gently, swirl your paints across the tank with a stylus, thin knitting needle or cocktail stick. You can make either large free swirls or more formal, regular ones.

1

MAKING A PRINT
Holding a sheet of paper by two opposite corners, carefully lay one corner on the surface of the paint and continue to lay the rest of the sheet in one smooth action.

2

Without pausing, pick up the two corners nearest you and carefully lift the paper out of the marbling tank.

DRYING

Lay the marbled sheet on plastic sheeting or newspaper, or hang up with clothes pegs and leave to drip dry. When dry, press under weights.

Projects

You can put your marbled paper to countless uses, and have lots of fun in the process. The projects that follow include a wide range of ideas, from making your own greetings cards and stationery, to a beautiful candleshade for your home. But, don't forget, these are only suggestions. With just a little imagination, the possibilities are, quite literally, endless!

Greetings cards

Marbled patterns on different weights of paper and card can be used to make attractive personalized cards and gift tags. The techniques for marbling on card are the same as for paper, but card is less malleable so you must be careful to lay it on the tank with exactly the right amount of pressure. You may find it easier to mount your marbled paper on card rather than marbling directly on the card itself. Three ideas are given below.

You will need:
- Ruler
  A choice of:
- 1 sheet of marbled paper and plain card (postcard weight) *or* Marbled card

- Cutting blade
- Tracing paper
- Newspaper
- Gold felt tip pen
- Hole punch (optional)
- Ribbon for gift tags (optional)
- Glue

Making marbled letters

This is a particularly amusing idea for young children. Glue the marbled paper on to fairly stiff card and leave to dry, or take a piece of marbled card. From a newspaper, trace the letters of your message on to the marbled side of the paper. Using a cutting blade, very carefully cut out the letters individually, taking care that the blade doesn't slip. Once the letters are cut out, you can give them to a child and let him/her put them together.

Making a card

Putting a marbled frame on a picture

Make gift tags to match your cards by folding marbled card in half, punching a hole in the corner and inserting some ribbon.

(Use marbled card or marbled paper glued to card.) Trim the marbled card to the size required, fold it in half firmly, then open it out flat. Cut a window out of the front and edge it with gold pen. Write a message inside the frame.

Take a piece of marbled paper the size of the print or photograph you will use. Cut out a window to make a frame. Fold a piece of plain card in half. Glue the picture to the front and leave to dry, then glue the marbled frame over the top.

*C*ard envelope and stationery

Edwardian ladies often used pretty card envelopes to keep their letters in. A marbled card envelope is easy to make and is useful for storing not only special letters, but photographs, handkerchiefs or stationery. Use pretty tinted papers for your letters, or make your own marbled stationery, taking care to make the marbling pale and light so that you will be able to read any writing on the paper. Simply keep the paints delicate by putting much less on the size than normal. Alternatively, you could always mask off a portion of the paper and just marble a border.

The instructions below are for an A5-sized envelope and A5 stationery. (You could also use A4 paper for the latter, but it will have to be folded.) The envelope can be made of marbled card or a sheet of marbled paper firmly glued to light card.

You will need:
A choice of:
- Marbled card *or*
- Sheet of marbled paper glued to card

- A5 envelope (for template)
- Pencil
- Scissors
- Cutting blade
- Length of ribbon 50cm (20in) long
- Glue
- A5 or A4 sheets of marbled paper (for stationery)

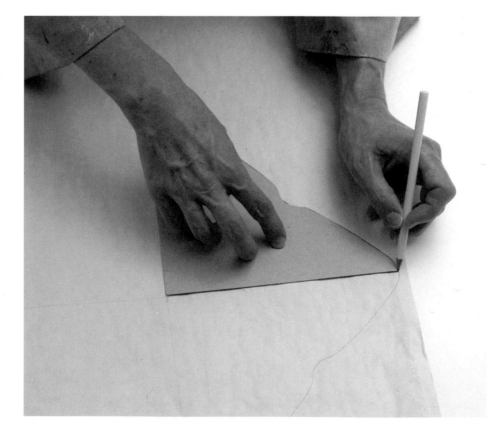

1 Unglue an A5 envelope and, with a pencil, trace around the shape on the back of your marbled card or paper.

2 *Carefully cut around the outline of the opened-out envelope with a pair of scissors.*

3 *Using your cutting blade, cut two slits, 2.5cm (1in) apart by 2.5cm (1in) long, in the middle of the card or paper for the ribbon.*

4 *Take the ribbon and thread it through the two slits which you have cut on the paper, with the two ribbon ends on the marbled side of the card. Following the creases on your template, fold and glue the three flaps into position.*

5 *Crease the final flap of the envelope firmly and fold it into shape.*

6 *Wrap the ribbon around the envelope and tie a bow above the flap to finish.*

The completed card envelope with stationery.

Candleshade

At the turn of the century, candles were still a major source of lighting, and were often adorned by charming shades which shed a gently diffused light. The fashion for candleshades has recently revived and marbled paper makes an excellent material. Choose your paper according to where you want the light to fall. Pale marbled paper will let some of the light glow through the shade, while darker paper will diffuse the light up and down.

A word of warning when making candleshades. It is obviously essential to make sure the flame does not come in contact with the paper. Bear in mind that the shade rests on a brass follower which, as the candle burns, will slowly glide down the candle, carrying the candleshade with it. It is therefore very important that the shade fits the follower exactly. The best way to ensure this is to measure the shade carefully so that it fits the follower exactly, and then double check by holding the two upside down. If your measurements are right, the shade should stay fixed to the follower. All commercially produced followers carry instructions and warnings, with advice about which type of candle to use. The shades below can also be used on electric candle bulbs – in which case, you will need to buy a brass electric adaptor to hold the shade over the bulb.

The instructions which follow are for a 10cm (4in) candleshade, which is an ideal size for use with either candles or bulbs.

You will need:
- Tracing paper

A choice of:
- Marbled card *or*
- Marbled paper ironed on to bonding card *or*
- Marbled paper bonded on to card with spray adhesive
- Pencil
- Cutting blade
- Felt tip pen
- Masking tape
- Brass follower
- Glue
- Clothes pegs

1 Using tracing paper, trace the diagram, which is exactly half size. Carefully repeat the right hand half by turning the pattern over. Do not repeat the seam allowance. Transfer the pattern to any one of the following: (a) marbled card, (b) marbled paper which has been ironed on to a proprietary brand of bonding card, or (c) marbled paper bonded on to card with spray adhesive. Draw around the template of your chosen alternative and cut out the shape.

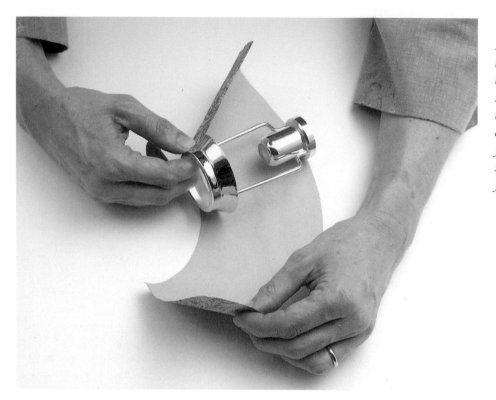

2 Using a colour of your choice, use a felt-tip pen to edge both the top and bottom of the shade. Join the side edges of the shade together with masking tape and try the shade on the follower to make absolutely sure that the shade is firmly fixed on to it.

3 Stick the sides of the shade together, gluing the overlap under its corresponding edge. Hold it in place with two clothes pegs until dry.

The completed candleshade.

Table mat and coasters

The table mat and coasters below will grace any table. Make them in matching or complementary colours. The instructions below are for straight-sided mats, since these are obviously much easier to cut out than round ones. You can, if you wish, cover the mat entirely with marbled paper, but there is a lot to be said for mounting a piece of marbled paper on card and painting a border around it, as described on page 74. It will protect the edges of the marbled paper from getting scuffed with time and use. To make the coasters, follow the instructions for the mat, using smaller pieces of card as required.

You will need:
- Marbled paper
- One piece of card, measuring 20 × 25cm (8 × 9in) (for the mat), plus required number of pieces of card measuring 11.5 × 8.5cm (4½ × 3½in) (for coasters)
- Pencil and ruler
- Paint
- Paintbrush
- Cutting blade
- Glue
- Heat-resistant varnish

Covering the mat with marbled paper

1 Edge the mat with gold paint. Use a ruler to make sure the line is completely straight and an even distance from the edge all round.

2 *Using a cutting blade, cut a piece of marbled paper just fractionally smaller all around than the size of the mat.*

3 *Glue the paper on the unmarbled side and press it down smoothly to remove any wrinkles or air bubbles. When the glue has dried, varnish the top and sides with two coats of varnish, checking to make sure that none of the brush bristles are left on the varnish.*

Using a border

1 First, decide how wide the border is going to be. Using a pencil and ruler, draw a border 2.5cm (1in) wide around the inside edges of the card. Using an undercoat if necessary, paint the whole border in a colour which complements your marbled paper. Leave to dry.

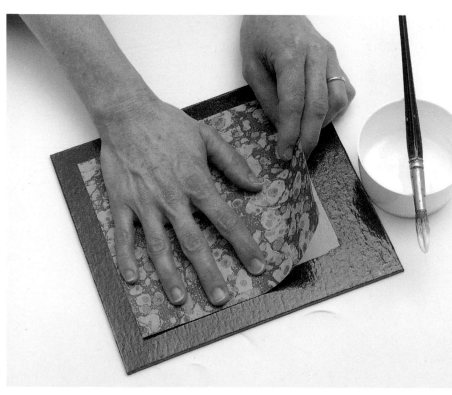

2 Meanwhile, cut the marbled paper into one piece measuring 18 × 20.5cm (7¼ × 8¼in) and glue the unmarbled side. Place the paper on the mat, being careful to get it absolutely straight. When the glue has dried, varnish the top and sides with two coats of varnish, checking to make sure that none of the brush bristles are left on the varnish.

The completed table mats and coaster.

Découpage

The first piece of découpage I ever saw was a black letter rack, smothered in a gorgeous design of primroses and bluebells which had been cleverly balanced by softly coloured flying birds. The decorative impact was nothing short of mouthwatering, while the finish on it was so perfect that I thought it had been hand-painted.

For years I made this black letter rack my yardstick and would not accept anything less perfect from either myself or my students until, one day, I saw an 18th-century Italian cupboard at a very prestigious antiques exhibition. It was decorated with a découpaged design, cut from contemporary hand-coloured prints. The paintwork, which was cream and turquoise, was in very reasonable condition considering its age, but the prints were badly cut out, very sketchily coloured, and had only the thinnest layer of varnish over them. What really amazed me, however, was that in spite of all this, the overall effect was absolutely fabulous.

A tremendous amount has been written about the perfect découpage technique, and, indeed, some of the projects in this book seek to attain the perfect finish. Since seeing that old cupboard, however, I am prepared to admit that if your design has some panache and style, nobody is going to miss .a few coats of varnish!

I am not saying that you should not cut out, colour and glue as well as you possibly can, but don't let the whole thing become such a chore that you cease to enjoy it. If you enjoy, and are truly enthusiastic about, what you are doing it gives the end result a certain glow and attractiveness.

HISTORY OF DÉCOUPAGE

If you look at the history of découpage, you will realize that you are continuing a craft that goes back at least as far as the 17th century. The craving for chinoiserie was at its height then, and it was extremely important to get a perfect finish, in order to emulate the hand-painted and highly lacquered furniture which was coming into Europe from the Orient.

For various reasons, this highly sought after furniture was arriving at far too slow a rate for the fashion-conscious. Luckily, the craftsmen of the day hit upon the comparatively speedy idea of hand-colouring prints with a Chinese theme, so that they could be cut out and stuck on to appropriately designed furniture. The prints were then sunk under layers of varnish until they were indistinguishable from freehand paintings.

As the same thing was also happening in Venice, découpage soon not only became an acceptable alternative to hand-painting, but also began to percolate through to the leisured classes as a new hobby.

Although we know that découpage was all the rage at the French court in the 1780s, I still find it very hard to imagine the likes of Marie Antoinette and her contemporaries slapping on coat after coat of varnish in their elaborate clothes and coiffures. I have a similar problem with the delicate wasp-waisted Victorian ladies, who are also known to have taken to découpage in a very big way – their specialities were huge screens covered in specially produced pictures called 'scraps'. What I would like to know is, Where did they actually do it? It must have been in the potting shed . . . they simply couldn't have laid about them with glue and varnish in the middle of all those stuffed birds and horsehair settees!

The thing is, I don't think that Marie Antoinette or the Victorians cared too much about how many coats of varnish their designs had. They just thoroughly enjoyed the whole process and it shows in the wonderful designs they produced.

I would like you to really enjoy découpage, too, and not to let yourself worry too much about the correctness of everything you do. If you want to go for a lacquer-like finish which has been achieved with 30 coats of varnish, that's wonderful, but if you are quite happy with the result you get after only two or three layers, just don't feel guilty about it! Remember, *you* are the designer!

Equipment and Techniques

Découpage equipment can be divided into two lists. The first – glue, paint and brushes, etc – can be bought in DIY stores. The second more enjoyable list includes unearthing unusual wrapping papers, prints, and interesting items to decorate.

There are no really difficult techniques in découpage – the secret for getting a good finish to your découpage is to make sure that you have everything you need before you start and that includes adequate space and plenty of time.

Equipment and materials

THE MOST OBVIOUS EQUIPMENT YOU WILL need, of course, is something to decorate. But this will present no problems, since almost anything can be découpaged, no matter what its age or what it's made from. My own particular preference is for old items, which I generally find in junk shops and at antique markets, but craft shops are also an excellent source for suitable wooden and cardboard objects such as the hat boxes in this book.

By using fabric instead of paper, découpage can be extended to decorating old wicker furniture as well as baskets, while there is no end to the 'potichomanie' you can do on glass plates, lamps and dishes. The possibilities are, literally, endless. Découpage can also be used to decorate walls, and there is no reason why you shouldn't also have a go at fitted furniture and floors. You could even rival the Sistine chapel and have a few angels flying around the ceiling!

Once you have decided what to découpage, you will then have to consider more specific equipment, as described below.

SOURCES FOR CUT-OUTS

Wrapping paper is so delicious nowadays, and usually of such good quality, that it is tempting to look no further, but there are so many other lovely designs tucked away in old children's books and gardening manuals – not to mention on calendars and posters – that if you keep your eyes open you can soon amass quite a collection.

There are also now several découpage resource books that provide a terrific selection of black-and-white and coloured prints, which you can either cut out and use as they are, or have photocopied, enlarged or reduced, to use over and over again.

You don't even have to stick to pictures, because decorative maps, calligraphy, hieroglyphics or border patterns are all usable in various ways, while the original, traditional Victorian paper scraps are actually being reprinted again and are quite widely available in a variety of shops.

Avoid cut-outs with heavy printing on the back of them. Although sealants will help a little, there is always a chance that the printing will show through and ruin your design.

BRUSHES

The golden rule for brushes is always to buy the best you can afford. You will be repaid by not having to stop constantly to fish out stray bristles from paint or varnish and by generally getting a much smoother finish.

House-painting brushes I use ordinary, 2.5cm (1in) to 4cm (1½in), house-painting brushes for all oil-based paints.

Squirrel mop brushes I use squirrel mop brushes for painting with emulsion paint. These take some getting used to initially, as they are very soft and seem to have no 'give', but they do leave a marvellously smooth finish.

Varnishing brushes You can buy special varnishing brushes, but they are expensive and a small house-painting brush will do just as well, especially if you buy the fattest and silkiest one you can find. Once you have designated a brush for varnishing, however, don't ever use it for anything else.

Artist's paintbrushes If you are going to use your brush with acrylic paints it is best to get one especially for this purpose, as acrylics are very hard on finer brushes such as sable. To mix up artist's oil colours use an artist's hoghair brush of a medium size.

GLUES

PVA glue is a flexible, reasonably fast-drying glue which dries to a clear finish. For this reason, as well as sticking on the cut-outs it can also be diluted and used as a varnish, a stiffener and to some extent as a sealant.

Wood glue I find that Evo-Stick Wood Adhesive is the answer to most wood sticking problems.

Spray adhesives are quick and very useful in some situations but on the whole I prefer the messier and more versatile PVA.

PAINTS, PRIMERS AND UNDERCOATS

Primers Use a wood primer on new or stripped wood to seal it and to prevent subsequent coats of paint from sinking into the grain. Give new unpainted metal or metal which has been stripped or rubbed back one or two coats of red oxide.

Undercoats It is always advisable to use an undercoat on new or stripped wood before applying the top coats. It is not always necessary if you are working on a sound painted or varnished surface, although it makes a useful first coat if you are painting on to a particularly intrusive colour.

Emulsion paints Emulsion paints are water-based and relatively quick-drying. Thinned down and built up in layers, they make a marvellous basis for découpage. They are porous, however, and need sealing with an acrylic sealant before being decorated.

Oil-based household paints Oil-based paints come in flat, eggshell and gloss finishes. Gloss paint is really not suitable for découpage, and in England oil-based flat paint has a very limited colour range which means that we are generally left with the eggshell or mid-sheen finish if we need to use an oil-based paint. Oil-based paints give a tougher finish than emulsions and I like to use them on pieces that are likely to get a lot of wear and tear. Their only disadvantage is that you must leave 24 hours between applications.

Artist's oil colours Artist's oil paints may be mixed with oil-based paints to tint them, but they are slow-drying and will slightly delay the drying time of the original paint. When used on their own to colour cracks or make antiquing fluid, it is best to leave the finish for at least a couple of days, even if it feels dry to the touch.

Artist's acrylic paints Artist's acrylic paints are usually bought in tubes, but now there are small pots of acrylic craft paints available, which come in a more fashionable range of colours and which you will find useful if you are not very good at mixing colours.

Acrylics are mixed with water and dry very quickly, although you can buy a retardant which will slow down the drying time a little. They are very useful for putting the finishing touches on pieces of découpage and may be applied over emulsion or oil-based paints.

Oil-based and watercolour pencils Either of these may be used for colouring prints although in the case of watercolour pencils, care must be taken not to get the print too wet as it will tend to buckle. Pencils are also very useful for repairing any accidental damage to prints which might occur during the rubbing-down process.

PAINT AND VARNISH STRIPPERS

Both are very caustic and are best put on with an old house-painting brush. Wear rubber gloves and make sure that you follow the instructions on the tin to the letter. The best type of tool to use is a pointed multi-edged paint scraper which is made specifically for the job, although with some tricky corners anything that gets a result is the best thing to use!

SANDPAPER, WIRE WOOL AND OTHER ABRASIVES

Sandpaper and wire wool are produced in all grades from very fine to coarse. They are used at all stages of découpage from smoothing the initial surface to rubbing down the final layer of varnish.

I also find abrasive cloths very useful, especially for rubbing down metal, and these are now readily available in most DIY stores.

You may prefer to use wet and dry abrasive papers for rubbing down wood, metal or oil-based paint surfaces but I do not advocate their wet use for an emulsion paint surface or for varnish that is covering prints, as it is difficult to see exactly what you are doing underneath all the 'slurry'.

SCALPELS, SCISSORS, CUTTING BOARDS AND ROLLERS

Scalpels There are dozens of craft knives on the market, some cheap and throwaway and others which have a long strip of push-up blades which snap off as you wish to change them. Most of these are not sharp enough or flexible enough for découpage. The best one to get is a slim metal scalpel with sharp renewable blades which you must change the *minute* they start getting blunt.

Scissors You will need a sharp curved pair of cuticle scissors and, once again, it is a question of buying the best you can afford. Sharpness is, of course, paramount, but you will also find that the

more expensive scissors are more comfortable. Comfort will definitely become a factor when you have been cutting out for an hour or two!

Cutting boards If you are using a scalpel to cut out your design you will need a cutting board of some kind. The very best are made in Japan and are designed so that they literally 'heal themselves' after you have cut on them. They are available in a variety of sizes from most good craft shops, but they are quite expensive.

Kitchen cutting boards or even old table mats make quite good alternatives, but you will have to stop using them as soon as they get scored or they will ruin your designs.

Rollers A little rubber roller is very useful for going over larger cut-outs in particular, as it ensures that no excess glue or air is trapped underneath and that everything is well and truly stuck down.

SEALANTS

Sealants have many uses. They are used on porous surfaces, such as emulsion paint or wood, to prevent subsequent layers of glue or varnish sinking in; also to fix and seal hand-coloured prints so that they do not run when they are glued and varnished. Finally, they are also used on all papers to make them less absorbent and to strengthen delicate designs during the cutting-out stage. Sealants are available in many forms. I find the acrylic spray-on variety the easiest to use.

TACK RAGS

Tack rags are lint-free extremely tacky cloths that will pick up all the dust and grit left behind by rubbing down with sandpaper, etc. They are very easy to get hold of now in builder's suppliers and will make all the difference to the finish of your work. Keep your tack rag in a jam jar with a screw lid and always shake it out well before using it. When using emulsion paint, use a lint-free rag wrung out in warm water as a tack rag.

VARNISHES

The good news about varnishing is that it is the crowning glory of découpage and, if well applied, gives it that wonderful, luminous hand-painted quality. The bad news is that most varnishes have a yellowing effect on the underlying surface, which can be disappointing if you have chosen or matched your colours with care.

Polyurethane and yacht varnish I rather like the mellowing effect that polyurethane and yacht varnishes give, and quite often emphasize it even more by antiquing the finished result. Polyurethane varnish will give you a really tough finish that will stand up to most household uses. It comes in a matt, satin, or gloss finish.

Yacht varnish is even tougher and for that reason has the most yellowing effect. It comes only in a gloss finish.

Acrylic varnish If you really want to keep as close to the original colours as possible, you may use an acrylic varnish, which, while it hardly discolours at all, is water-based and usually needs at least one coat of yacht or polyurethane varnish to give it a tough enough finish for tables and trays etc. Acrylic varnish generally comes in a gloss or eggshell finish.

Crackle varnish gives your work a really cracked and ancient look, which looks particularly good over more classical designs. It is quite easy to obtain from most art shops and comes in a pack containing one bottle of slow-drying varnish, which is usually tinted to give an even more antique effect, and one bottle of fast-drying varnish.

WAX

A final coat or two of clear wax polish gives a lovely deep sheen to most pieces, particularly if you have used a matt or satin finish varnish. I wax polish my work as often as possible and the surface just goes on getting better and better. Polishing with a good-quality tinted wax will also give your work quite a passable antiqued finish.

WHITE SPIRIT AND METHYLATED SPIRIT

White spirit is a substitute for turpentine and may be used to dilute any oil-based paint and as a solvent for removing oil paint and polyurethane varnish from clothes and brushes etc. It may also be used with wire wool for rubbing down and cleaning old pieces which are about to be painted.

Methylated spirits may be used with wire wool for rubbing down and cleaning. This combination is also useful for removing sticky layers of french polish.

WOOD FILLERS

Most quick-drying wood fillers will be suitable for anything that you are likely to come across. If you are dealing with very fine cracks, small holes or rough grain, you will find fine surface polyfiller very useful.

Basic techniques

IT'S ALWAYS POSSIBLE TO BUY A NEW wooden or metal object to découpage and to get straight on with priming and painting. But if you can find an old piece with character your découpage will look a lot more exciting and authentic. However, there is always a down side to everything and I'm afraid that if you are going for authenticity, before the delicious tasks of applying colours and designs can begin, the more mundane jobs of stripping, rubbing down and filling must be tackled.

Although these jobs come pretty low on most people's list of favourite things, it can in fact be very satisfying to restore a rickety, battered and heavily painted old piece to its smooth, glued and

wooden or metal origins, before indulging in the ultimate pleasure of applying a completely new set of finery.

STRIPPING

If you have a reasonably unbroken surface on the piece you wish to decorate, it is not always necessary to strip it, but if the paint or varnish is chipped and uneven, then it is a good idea to take it all off and start from scratch.

Basically, you have two choices when it comes to stripping: doing it yourself or taking it to a commercial strippers. The decision usually rests on how much money you wish to spend and/or how big the piece is. Taking the piece to a commercial stripper usually costs a lot more than doing it yourself, although, if it's a really big piece, it will certainly be a lot quicker – and they will usually collect and deliver to your door.

Stripping at home

Stripping even small things at home can lead to chaos if you do not make adequate preparations. Stripping isn't difficult in itself, but you do have to lock up any livestock, *including* small children, and make sure that everything which might get splashed is covered in a layer or two of newspaper. You yourself should wear an apron and a pair of rubber gloves.

There are several good makes of stripper available which are suitable for either metal or wood, although you need to make sure that you get the correct one, depending on whether you are removing varnish or paint.

Incidentally, it is very easy to confuse a varnished surface with one that has been french-polished. If you are not sure, try rubbing a small corner of the surface with some fine wire wool soaked in methylated spirits. If you are in fact dealing with

STRIPPING OFF PAINT

When using paint-stripper wear rubber gloves and make sure you follow the instructions on the tin to the letter. The best type of tool to use is a pointed multi-edged paint scraper.

french polish you will find that your wire wool will soon be clogged with a brown sticky mess and you can continue to clean the rest of the french polish off with fresh applications of wire wool and methylated spirit.

If the surface has been varnished you will only remove the surface dirt with the wire wool and you will need to use a stripper specifically for varnished surfaces. Whichever type of surface you are removing, follow the instructions on the bottle carefully and leave to dry.

Commercial stripping

If you do decide to go for the commercial stripping option, you will find, once again, that you have a choice: between the caustic and the non-caustic methods of stripping. There is quite a big difference between these two methods, in terms of both the actual process and the cost.

As usual you get what you pay for, and you will find that the more expensive non-caustic method is the safest for anything delicate, such as pieces with gesso decoration or inlay, while the caustic method is more suitable for chunky pine pieces or cheap old 'horrors' that you don't want to spend a fortune on.

Cleaning a sound surface prior to painting

If the surface you are going to decorate is absolutely sound, it will not need stripping, but it will need cleaning to remove any wax and dirt that might have collected over the years.

To remove wax, go over the whole piece with wire wool, soaked in white spirit. Rub with the grain wherever possible and renew the wire wool as and when it gets dirty. If you are quite sure that there is no wax or polish on the surface, you may just wipe it over with a cloth wrung out in hot soapy water. Be careful not to drench the piece in water, however, as this will raise the grain of the wood and give you even more rubbing down to do!

GLUING AND FILLING

If you have any bits to glue back or holes to fill, this is the time to attend to them. As you may imagine, almost anything can happen to a piece of furniture over the years and it would not be appropriate to deal with all the calamities here. However, for relatively simple problems such as replacing missing beading or re-uniting split panelling you will need a good-quality wood adhesive and clamps, pins, or even a heavy book or masking tape to hold the pieces together while they dry.

FILLING HOLES AND CRACKS

After cleaning old wooden furniture, fill in any holes with wood filler. When dry, rub down, first with medium sandpaper, then with fine, then 'dust' with a tack rag.

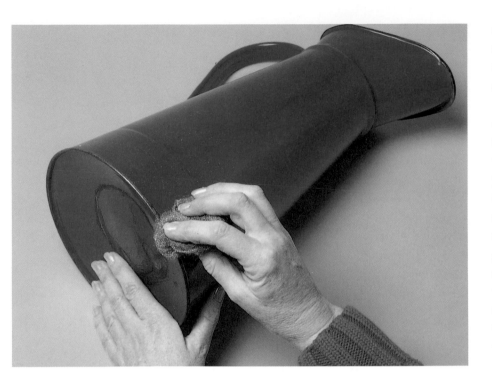

RUBBING WITH FINE WIRE WOOL
*When you first start rubbing away you won't believe that it
is possible to remove all the rust. Five minutes later you
may still not believe it. But you can and you must!*

Holes and dents can be filled with either wood
filler or fine surface polyfiller if the dent is shallow
enough. Fine surface polyfiller can also be used to
give a smooth surface to a particularly rough-
grained piece of wood or the rough ends of man-
made boards, such as chipboard.

RUBBING DOWN
Whether your piece needs stripping or whether
you are retaining the original surface, what you
do next is of the utmost importance, because if
you don't make sure that you have a beautifully
smooth surface at this point, you won't stand a

chance of ending up with a perfect piece of
découpage, and all the painstaking work still to
come will be wasted and made more difficult as
a result.

Having thoroughly unnerved you with my last
comment let me tell you exactly how to achieve
this beautifully smooth finish. First, when working
with wood, always use a sanding block wherever
possible. Then, with sandpaper wrapped around
this, sand with long firm strokes, using the whole
of your arm and shoulder and always going with
the grain. Alternatively, you may prefer to use a
good handful of very fine wire wool. I use fine
sandpaper on biggish flat pieces and 'ribbons' of
wire wool for tricky pieces like turned legs and
awkward corners. I also find the fine abrasive cloths
which are available now very flexible for anything
with a rounded edge.

If you are decorating a metal piece, some of these
cloths are made specifically for metal and are
particularly useful, although very fine wire wool
will also give metal a wonderful surface.

If your metal piece is old it will almost certainly
have developed some rust spots, which the stripping
process will not remove entirely. Treat these with a
rust remover and bash away with a piece of fine
wire wool, until all traces of rust have been
removed.

You may be tempted, especially on a large item,
to use an electric sander, but unless you are
particularly adept with it, I strongly advise you to
resist the temptation as it is only too easy to overdo
it and end up with disfiguring whirls in the wood,
and horribly burred edges on the metal.

Whichever method you use to achieve your
smooth surface, all will soon be lost if you do not
make sure that you have cleaned away every speck
of sawdust, etc., before continuing with the next
stage.

The best way of ensuring a dust-free surface is to wipe it over carefully with a tack rag. These are quite easy to obtain in builder's suppliers or even DIY shops and are just what they sound, lint-free and extremely tacky rags.

Make sure that you always replace tack rags in their container when you have finished with them and that you always give them a good shake before you use them again and they will last for ages. If by any chance you cannot track one down, any lint-free rag, wrung out in turpentine (if you are using oil-based paints) or warm water (if you are using emulsions) will make a reasonable substitute.

PRIMING AND PAINTING

Priming metal

If you are working on old metal you will have removed any trace of rust by now, during the rubbing-down process, but to ensure that your piece remains rust-free you will need to prime it with two coats of red oxide before going any further.

If you are working on new tin, remove any superficial grease with hot soapy water and give the surface a slight key, or roughness, by rubbing it down with fine wire wool. Dry it well before applying red oxide.

Priming wood

If you are working on a rubbed-down surface that has already been painted or varnished there will be no need to apply primer but you will need to apply wood primer to anything that has been stripped or to new wood.

APPLYING THE BASE COAT

Painting with water-based paints

It is very difficult to say what the traditional base coat for découpage is. Nowadays you can find

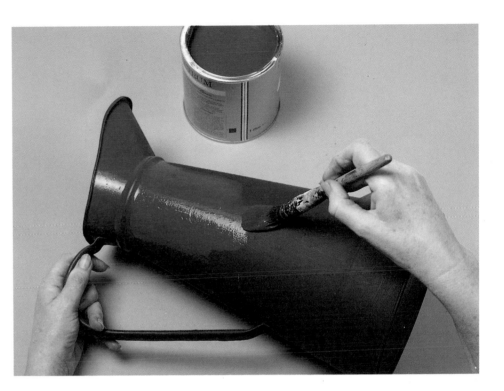

PRIMING WITH RED OXIDE

Prime a metallic surface with two coats of red oxide, inside and out. When dry, lightly rub down and tack, then apply coats of thinned-down emulsion paint and acrylic sealant.

instructions that include only one coat of paint, which is quite reasonable when you learn that 18th-century découpers were known to stick their designs directly on to pasteboard.

I have always thought of the following method as being the traditional one. It is certainly the method which gives the most beautiful effect, although, I have to admit, it is also the one which requires the greatest amount of patience.

Decant some emulsion paint into a clean jam jar and dilute it with a little water (about a tablespoonful of water to half an average-sized jar). Stir the mixture well before applying it to the piece to be decorated, using a squirrel haired mop if possible (see 'Brushes', page 80). If it is a wooden piece, paint in the same direction as the grain wherever possible, taking care to put on a thin even coat of paint. Check for drips and leave to dry.

Initially, you may put on two or even three of these thinned-down coats of paint before rubbing down gently with fine sandpaper and going over the piece with your tack rag. Repeat this entire process, rubbing down and tacking between coats, until you have built up a smooth, even surface as close to alabaster as you can get!

Depending upon the make of paint you are using and your own personalized version of diluting . . .

COLOURING A PRINT

First apply the colour with watercolour pencils, then spread it with a damp brush so that it resembles watercolour. Be careful not to wet the print too much or it will buckle.

this will probably involve between six and ten coats of paint. Finish by gently rubbing down and tacking.

Painting with oil-based paints

I use oil-based paints as a base coat when I am doing a piece that is likely to get a lot of use and where emulsion paint would be more likely to chip. The best paint to use is one with a satin or eggshell finish and, generally speaking, it is not necessary to dilute it, although if you do need to, use the same method as for water-based paints, substituting turpentine or white spirit for water.

Use an ordinary 2.5cm (1in) or 4cm (1½in) house-painting brush and, as with emulsions, paint wherever possible in the direction of the grain.

You will find that oil-based paints take much longer to dry and that you will not usually need to apply more than three or four coats to achieve a good smooth surface. You will need to rub down and tack after each coat.

You will find that I often say rub down 'gently' and 'lightly' in the projects. This is because once you have achieved your smooth surface prior to painting, all other rubbing down is simply to remove any slight irregularities, such as dust or brush marks. If you rub too hard, you will be back to the wood.

COLOURING A PRINT

Nowadays, it is only too easy to go out and buy a couple of sheets of good-quality wrapping paper to cut out for découpage, but in previous centuries, découpers used prints for their designs, some of which had to be coloured before they could be used.

If you want to try your hand at colouring a print, first make sure that the print you have in mind is of no great value or, better still, acquire one of the excellent découpage resource books which are available now. These contain dozens of copies of the original coloured and uncoloured prints so that you can really make your piece look antique.

For colouring, use good-quality oil-based pencils so that you can mix them for maximum effect and aim for plenty of variety in tone, leaving small amounts of white uncovered to keep the picture lively. It is not a good idea, however, to be too subtle because very delicate colours will not show to advantage under several coats of varnish.

You will find that your pencils cover better and that you will have more control over graduations if you use shortish strokes packed close together. When you wish to grade a colour gradually from light to dark, let longer and shorter strokes gently dovetail into one another where the light starts to merge into the dark. You will also get a more uniform effect if you keep your strokes going in the same direction as the original shading strokes on the print.

When you have completed the colouring stage of your print and before you cut it out, you will need to spray the right side sparingly with sealant (page 82) and leave it to dry.

If you are using watercolour pencils, apply the colour dry in the usual way, spreading it with a damp brush so that it resembles watercolour. Take care not to wet the print excessively, or it will buckle.

CUTTING OUT AND ARRANGING
YOUR DESIGN

This is where the fun really begins, and I can honestly say that I know people who have become seriously addicted to the leisurely pursuit of cutting out designs for découpage.

There are two ways of cutting: with a scalpel or with a small curved pair of cuticle scissors. I use both, depending on the intricacy of the design. There is nothing like a pair of scissors for swooping

around the curved petals of a flower, but a scalpel is wonderful for tackling straight edges and slim stems.

Whichever method you decide upon, you will also need a larger pair of scissors to cut the print or paper into manageable pieces. Don't, for example, attempt to cut a tiny flower straight out of a whole sheet of wrapping paper.

If you are using a scalpel, work on a cutting board (page 82) and wherever possible move the paper rather than the knife, which should be cutting towards you. If using scissors, you will find it easier to work with your cutting hand under the paper, with your other hand moving the paper into position as you cut.

CUTTING WITH A SCALPEL

If you are using a scalpel, work on a cutting board and whenever possible move the paper rather than the knife, which should be cutting towards you.

<u>CUTTING WITH SCISSORS</u>
Small scissors are perfect for cutting out the swirling shapes of these flowers, but use the larger ones for cutting the paper into more manageable pieces.

Always cut the small 'inner' pieces of background away first, leaving the outside contours until near the end and also leaving any flimsy, delicate pieces well supported by adjacent background until the very last minute.

As you cut each piece, store it carefully where it cannot get lost or creased, until you are ready to plan your design. I keep my cut-outs in flat, plastic display pages, so that I can see what they are and check that they are not creased, but putting them between the pages of a book does just as well.

When you are sure that you have cut out enough for your design, arrange the pieces on the article

to be decorated and fix them temporarily in place with Blu-Tack. It's as well to give some thought to your design at this stage because you will have already spent a lot of time in the preparation of this piece and you have more to do yet. It would be a shame to spoil it all by just plonking the design on anywhere.

Avoid scattering design elements all over the piece in a haphazard manner, for example, but try to give some kind of focal point to the design and tie any other sections to this, either by use of colour or similarity.

Above all, if you have a strong feeling that the whole thing would all fall into place if only you had a tree to put here or a few birds to scatter there . . . go out and find them and then get cutting! You will never be truly happy with the design if you don't.

GLUING
There are two methods of gluing advocated by découpers. One involves spreading small amounts of glue on to the object before laying each design piece into place and the other is simply to glue the back of the paper cut-out before arranging it in its predestined place.

There are advantages and drawbacks to both methods but, on the whole, unless you are creating a very intricate design, I think I prefer the second. I use an old melamine chopping board to glue on so that I can wash it down frequently between pieces, but you can also use pieces of aluminium kitchen foil and throw them away when they get too sticky.

If you are gluing on to an emulsioned surface, a slight spray with sealant (page 82) will make the surface less porous and give you more time to arrange your design. As you glue each piece down it is important to make sure that it is absolutely smooth and that all the edges are well stuck down. I usually go over larger cut-outs with a rubber roller to squeeze out any air bubbles or deposits of excess glue and then I clean up any spare glue with a soft cloth, which has previously been wrung out in warm water. Next, I go around the edges of each piece, pressing them down firmly with a glue-free fingertip. (I find it simpler to dispense with the roller for smaller, more fragile cut-outs and just use clean fingers and the cloth to smooth them down.) Finally I check, yet again, that all the edges and especially any spiky bits are well and truly stuck down.

ARRANGING THE DESIGN
Arrange the paper cut-outs on the piece and attach the Blu-Tack. Remember that the piece has to look good from all sides, so be careful of any trailing bits that might creep round and turn up where you do not want them.

GLUING THE DESIGN
As you glue each piece down, make sure it is absolutely smooth and that all the edges are well stuck down. I usually go over larger cut-outs with a rubber roller to squeeze out any excess glue and then clean up any spare glue with a soft cloth, wrung out in warm water.

Should you find a loose edge that has previously missed your eagle eye, take a small amount of glue on the end of a cocktail stick, and slide it under the paper, holding it down for a second or two with your fingertip.

When you are quite happy that the design is safely battened down, check for any tell-tale shiny areas of excess glue. If you find any, wash them away carefully with a soft cloth or small piece of sponge wrung out in fairly warm water.

VARNISHING

The aim when varnishing a piece of découpage is to completely submerge the design, so that if you were to run your finger across the surface of your work you would not be able to detect the edges of the paper cut-outs. As you can imagine, it takes a great many layers of varnish to achieve this state of affairs, but, as I said in the introduction, it is for you to decide where you wish to stop.

Although drips and runs need to be avoided at all costs, varnish should be applied to the surface in generous strokes before being brushed out lightly across the original brush strokes. With

VARNISHING THE DESIGN
Apply two coats of varnish, leaving 24 hours between each. Rub down and tack. Apply at least six more coats of varnish, rubbing down and tacking between each. Give one more light rubbing down and wax.

polyurethane varnishes you need not rub down and tack until after the second or third coat has dried and with water-based varnishes you may complete three or four coats before it becomes necessary. After that, though, you must rub down and tack *very* lightly after every coat.

Don't forget, especially with the early layers, that the vulnerable paper cut-outs are only just beneath the surface. If you do happen to catch one with the sandpaper, it will leave a glaringly white mark, which you can usually disguise by smudging on some oil-based or watercolour pencils. You will need to seal the repair with a spray of acrylic sealant, but then you can go on varnishing as usual.

WAXING AND ANTIQUING

When you have applied your final coat of varnish you may well let out a huge sigh of relief and leave it at that, but you can, if you like, go on and give your work an antiqued or waxed surface, or even both. Whichever it is, you will first need to give the surface a slight key by rubbing it down lightly with fine wire wool or sandpaper.

Waxing

Basically, this is just a question of getting a good wax polish and following the instructions on the tin, but you know what they say . . . to get that really deep gleam you need to wax every day for a week, every week for a month and every month for a year . . . at least! (You can, incidentally, also get quite a passable antiqued finish by applying a tinted wax instead of the usual clear variety.)

Creating a plain antiqued finish

You will need (for a small to medium-sized item) *Raw Umber artist's oil paint · Black artist's oil paint · white spirit · jam jar · artist's paintbrush · 2 small house-painting brushes · some old nylon stockings or tights*

1. Squeeze into the bottom of the jam jar approximately 2.5cm (1in) of Raw Umber oil paint and about 6mm (¼in) of the Black. Add a little of the white spirit and mix into a smooth creamy paste with the artist's paintbrush. Gradually add a little more white spirit until your mixture is slightly thinner than single cream.

2. Using one of the house-painting brushes, paint this mixture over the entire piece, poking it well into any nooks and crannies and especially around locks or handles.

3. Leave the antiquing until it has lost all its gloss but has not dried and then, with a clean cloth in your free hand, take a clean, dry, house-painting brush and work the antiquing well into the surface while at same time gradually removing a large portion of it. Keep wiping the brush on the cloth as you work and stop when your design begins to show through quite clearly.

4. Cut the nylon tights or stockings into pieces and form each piece into a wad. Take one of these and rub the surface in a circular motion.

Your imagination and artistry need to come into play now as you rub more of the antiquing off where the item might have got worn over the years, and leave more of it on where dirt might have collected. Changing the nylon wads as they get dirty, continue to work in a circular motion emphasizing some parts of the design by rubbing off more of the antiquing fluid and leaving other parts more obscure by leaving it fairly dark. When you are quite happy with the effect, leave the antiquing until it is completely dry before protecting it with a coat of varnish.

Creating a 'crackle' varnish finish

If you use the ready-made variety of crackle varnish and follow the instructions *carefully*, you should succeed.

You will find two bottles in the packet you buy. The first one is an oil-based, and usually antiqued, varnish which you paint on first and allow to dry to the point of tackiness. You then paint on the second varnish which is water-based and fast-drying. The cracks appear on the surface after the second coat has dried because the oil-based coat is still drying and on the move.

When everything has dried out, add a little more white spirit to the recipe for antiquing (above) and paint this over the whole thing. Leave for two minutes then wipe off all the excess colour with a soft cloth. Allow to dry thoroughly and finish with a coat of varnish.

ANTIQUING – RUBBING THE FLUID BACK
When the fluid has dulled, take a clean paintbrush and work it into the wood. Make a wad from a piece of nylon and begin to rub the antiquing off a little, taking more off where there would have been a lot of action.

Projects

I love the 'transformation scene' that comes at the
end of pantomimes when everyone and
everything is revealed in all their glory. I had the
same kind of feeling when I was painting
up and découpaging the old and decrepit pieces
in these projects.

If, however, you do not share my penchant for rags
to riches, there are plenty of new items to
decorate, such as cardboard hat boxes. These
are available in a variety of shops and have
the advantage of being easy to find.

Mirror

Butterflies, bugs and birds are so useful for balancing designs or tying elements together that I seldom make a design without one or other of them. It was like that with this mirror, which I decided to decorate for use in a nursery, mainly because I had been longing to use these gorgeous Lawson Wood illustrations.

Preparing
You will need:
- Wood filler
- Medium and fine sandpaper
- Tack rag
- Wooden knob for the drawer
- Wood glue
- Wood primer
- Oil-based eggshell paint
- Brushes
- White spirit (to thin brushes)

Decorating
You will need:
- Paper cut-outs
- Blu-Tack
- PVA glue
- Soft lint-free cloth
- Roller
- Polyurethane clear varnish
- Brushes
- Antiquing materials (page 92)
- Wax

It didn't matter how I put the pictures on to the frame, however, the design always seemed to lack unity, until I found the little butterflies, which were small and dark and didn't detract from the illustrations, but whose wandering presence tied the whole thing together.

PREPARING THE MIRROR
There was a thick coat of badly applied paint on the mirror when I bought it, which I had stripped off commercially. The stripping revealed all sorts of cracks and holes which had previously been bunged-up with paint and which needed filling with wood filler.

Once the filler had dried out, the whole thing needed rubbing down, first with medium sandpaper and then with fine. It was then gone over with a tack rag.

I also fitted a new wooden knob to the drawer at this point, which necessitated drilling a hole before gluing the knob into place. Taking care to rub down and tack between each coat, I then gave the mirror two coats of primer followed by three coats of paint, leaving 24 hours between each application.

DECORATING THE MIRROR
I arranged and re-arranged the paper cut-outs on the mirror frame with Blu-Tack, until I was happy with the design. I then removed each piece singly, pasted it with glue and returned it to its place. The small pieces I pressed into place with a clean fingertip and a cloth wrung out in warm water,

1 *There was a thick coat of badly applied paint on the mirror when I bought it, which I had stripped off commercially.*

The Art & Craft of Paper

but I went over the larger ones with the roller, to squeeze out any excess glue.

When everything was dry, I double-checked for any loose corners or spots of dried glue, which I restuck or wiped off with the warm damp cloth.

I then gave the whole thing eight coats of varnish, rubbing down and tacking very lightly after every coat except the first one.

When the last coat of varnish was dry, I antiqued (see page 92) the mirror and left it to dry for a few days before giving it a final coat of varnish, followed the next day by an application of wax (see page 92).

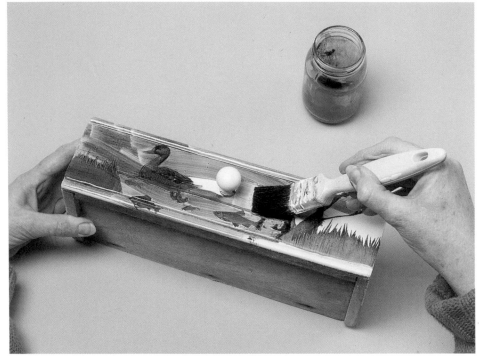

2 The stripping revealed all sorts of cracks and holes which had previously been bunged up with paint and which I filled with wood filler.

3 To achieve an antiqued look, I painted on a generous coating of antiquing fluid, making sure to push it into all the nooks and crannies. I then left it until it began to dull.

4 When the fluid had dulled, I took a clean paintbrush and worked it into the wood, especially where any real dirt would have gathered over the years. Finally, I made a smooth ball from a piece of nylon and began to rub the antiquing off a little, taking more off in places where there would have been a lot of action – around the drawer knob, for example.

Doll's cradle

I pity the poor old doll who slept in this cradle. When I bought it it was painted heavily with the foulest pink paint and was absolutely bristling with round-headed screws.

I was so keen to get rid of the awful pink paint that I took it to the strippers on my way home from buying it. Imagine my horror when I returned some days later, only to find that the paint had been of the old and tenacious 'nursery' variety, which was never actually *meant* to come off . . . ever!

Preparing
You will need:
- Coarse sandpaper
- Wood filler
- Fine sandpaper
- Tack rag
- Wood primer
- Brushes
- White oil-based eggshell paint
- White paper
- White spirit (to clean brushes)
- Artist's oil paints (Ultramarine and Raw Umber)
- Small rectangular piece of varnished glass

Decorating
You will need:
- Paper cut-outs
- Blu-Tack
- PVA glue
- Roller
- Soft lint-free cloth
- Polyurethane clear varnish
- Brushes

The stripper had done his best but there still remained a thin layer of the dreaded colour which I rubbed down and covered up as soon as I possibly could.

When I had dealt with the screws and repainted it, the cradle had such a pretty old-fashioned shape that I found modern pictures just didn't look right on it while these drawings of Edwardian children playing in the park seem to suit it exactly.

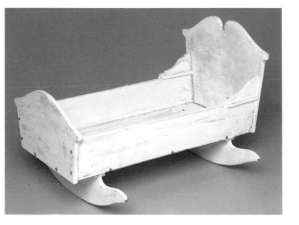

2 To make this soft lavender blue I have mixed about 2.5cm (1in) of Ultramarine artist's oil paint and just a touch of Raw Umber with enough white spirit to mix them to a creamy consistency. I then gradually added the white eggshell paint until I arrived at the correct colour.

PREPARING THE DOLL'S CRADLE

When something has been stripped as rigorously as this has you will find that the grain of the wood will be slightly lifted (more so if you have used the caustic method [see page 85]). You might therefore have to rub the piece down a little with coarse sandpaper to see where it needs filling.

I did this, then filled all holes, cracks and

1 Believe it or not but there were 36 round-headed screws poking out of this one little doll's cradle when I bought it. These all had to be removed and replaced with counter sunk, flat-headed screws and the holes filled and rubbed down before anything else could be done.

abrasions with wood filler and left it to dry. I then rubbed it down with fine sandpaper until the cradle was smooth, and wiped it with a tack rag (see page 87). I then applied primer according to the instructions on the tin and left it to dry, before rubbing it down lightly and tacking.

I then mixed up the colour for the base coat (page 87) and smeared a little of the mixed colour on a piece of white paper. I viewed the result through a piece of varnished glass, to see what the final effect would be and made any necessary adjustments. I used this base colour to apply three or four coats to the cradle, remembering to rub down and tack between each application. I left 24 hours between coats (don't be tempted to go any faster as you have already added extra oil to the mixture which will slow the drying time) before applying the design. I then rubbed it down very lightly to give a slight key and tacked the whole thing.

DECORATING THE DOLL'S CRADLE

I arranged the design on the cradle, using Blu-Tack to hold it in place. Then I glued the design in position, using my fingers and the roller to squeeze any excess glue out from under the paper. I then wiped off any spare glue with the soft cloth wrung out in warm water.

I checked that each piece was well stuck down before going on to the next by pressing firmly around the edges with the tip of my finger.

When I had completed the design, I restuck loose ends with a little glue on a cocktail stick.

Before varnishing, I checked for any shiny patches of dried, excess glue and wiped them off with a cloth wrung out in hot water.

I then applied two coats of polyurethane clear varnish, leaving 24 hours between each application. After that I rubbed down gently, taking care not to rub so hard that I scuffed the design.

I went over the cradle once more with the tack rag and continued to varnish, rub down and tack until I had sunk the edges of the design.

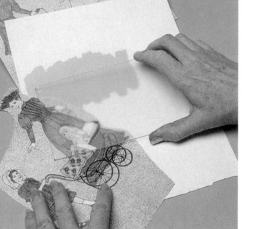

3 When using so many layers of polyurethane varnish it is inevitable that the original colours will yellow. This is not always a bad thing as it can have a harmonizing effect but as you are mixing your own colour for this project, you can, as I did, look through the varnished glass and make adjustments.

4 Once you have begun to varnish, anything that is not really stuck down will become a problem, so get used to checking and then double checking!

Hat box

I love hat boxes almost as much as I love hats but, although I've got several of them decorated in various styles, I think that this one is my favourite. It is decorated in the traditional Victorian manner with a multitude of overlapping 'scraps', which are little embossed pictures depicting a variety of subjects, from wild life to the high fashion of Victorian times, when they were first published.

Preparing

You will need:
- Cardboard hat box base
- Acrylic sealant
- 2–3 sheets of darkish wrapping paper
- Pencil
- Scissors
- Ruler
- PVA glue
- Soft lint-free cloth
- Roller

Decorating

You will need:
- Several sheets of scraps
- Small curved scissors
- Blu-Tack
- PVA glue
- Soft lint-free cloth
- Polyurethane clear varnish
- House-painting brush
- Fine sandpaper
- Tack rag

Luckily for us, the original scraps are being reproduced again today and are usually available in most good craft outlets, together with the cardboard bases for the hat boxes.

1 These cardboard hat boxes are a godsend to découpers and hoarders alike. They come in at least four sizes and, once decorated, make beautiful containers for all sorts of vital junk.

PREPARING THE HAT BOX
- As the hat box is made from cardboard it is a good idea to give it a spray with acrylic sealant so that the glue will not be absorbed too quickly when you are sticking on the base paper.
- While the spray is drying, lay the lid of the box upside down on the reverse side of a piece of wrapping paper and draw round it lightly with a pencil.
- Carefully draw a second circle approximately 2.5cm (1in) outside the first circle. You will have to do this freehand so don't worry if it wobbles a bit.
- Cut around the freehand pencil line with scissors, so that you end up with a circle of wrapping paper with a pencil circle drawn 2.5cm (1in) in from the outside edge.

- Working around the edge of the circle, cut in to the pencil line at intervals of about 2.5cm (1in).
- Repeat this process, using the base of the hat box. Mark the base with a small 'b' as the two pieces look very similar in size but are significantly different.
- Measure the length and depth of the circumference of the lid and cut out a piece of wrapping paper which is the same length but 2.5cm (1in) deeper than this.
- Draw a pencil line 2.5cm (1in) from the edge of this piece of paper and along the length.
- Working along this edge, cut in to the pencil line at approximately 2.5cm (1in) intervals.
- Repeat this process to cut a piece of paper to fit the sides of the base of the hat box, remembering to leave 2.5cm (1in) to spare on the depth.

• Paste the back of the circle of paper reserved for the lid with glue and place it on to the outside of the lid so that the fringed edge is sticking out all round.

• Using a cloth wrung out in warm water, smooth the paper on to the lid, working out from the middle and making sure that there are no pockets of excess glue, creases or air bubbles. Finally, go over it with a roller.

• Check that the underside of the fringed edge is still well covered in glue and then work around the edge of the lid pressing down every other tab. Repeat with the second lot of alternate tabs so that they slightly overlap the first.

• Repeat this process with the second circle to cover the bottom of the hat box.

• Paste the back of the strip reserved for the edge of the lid and glue it around the outside of the circumference so that the fringed edge can be bent over and glued inside the lid, using the same method as before.

• Do the same with the strip reserved for the sides of the base, pasting the fringed edge inside the box, once more.

• Be especially careful to keep the sides of the box smooth by wiping the paper with the cloth as you fit it around the box.

DECORATING THE HAT BOX

Although the scraps are partly cut out you will still need to trim them and cut out some small background pieces here and there.

• When you have had a good look through your collection and trimmed them, choose a few of the larger ones to make the centre piece of your design. Although this type of découpage looks random, you still need some kind of master plan.

• It isn't practical to Blu-Tack every scrap on to the hat box before you start gluing but it is a good idea to fix the major elements in place to remind yourself about which pieces you wish to remain dominant, otherwise they can get swamped underneath a lot of little scraps.

• When you have the main elements Blu-Tacked, you can start gluing your scraps on, making sure that you press each one in place with a cloth wrung out in warm water and checking that all the edges are completely stuck down. (This is the one form of découpage where it is permissible to allow the scraps to overlap and you will also find that, if you have chosen your base paper wisely, it will not matter if you occasionally leave a *small* gap.)

• When you have completely covered the outside of the hat box with scraps, apply four coats of varnish, leaving 24 hours between each application.

• After the fourth coat is dry, sand the whole thing *very* lightly and tack (see page 87), but remember that with this kind of découpage you are dealing with an uneven surface and you must therefore be extremely careful not to rub too hard, when

2 *I was lucky enough to find a base paper which was actually decorated with Victorian scraps. If you can't find anything similar, any darkish paper will do, providing that it has a light-coloured reverse side so that you can draw and cut accurately.*

Lining

You will need:

- 2 sheets of wrapping paper
- Pencil
- Scissors
- Ruler
- PVA glue
- Soft lint-free cloth
- Acrylic sealant
- Matt varnish

3 *Scraps usually come, partly cut out, in sheet form and will still need trimming and tidying up a little.*

sanding, or you will catch the scraps and ruin them. If you do have a mishap of this kind, try and repair the damage with oil-based coloured pencils softened into the original print with the tip of your finger. Fix the repair with sealant and continue varnishing but don't forget that this particular spot will be very vulnerable every time you sand.

- It is up to you how many coats of varnish you apply from now on but, ideally, you should not be able to feel the edges of the scraps when you have finished. This will take at least 20 more coats of varnish with sanding and tacking in between.

I know that the temptation to stop after a few more coats is very strong, but patience is a virtue and if you do press on, your reward will be the awesome sight of the scraps glowing deeply from beneath layers and layers of mellow varnish.

LINING THE HAT BOX

- Place the lid and the base on the wrong side of the wrapping paper and draw around both.
- Cut out the circles and mark them lightly so that you know which is which.
- Cut out two strips for the sides of the base and lid, following the instructions for the outside.
- Fold the fringed edge of the base strip back towards the right side of the paper and crease well.
- Straighten out the paper and apply a good coat of glue before fitting the strip inside the base so that the fringed edge is bent and pasted onto the floor of the box. Use the same technique for fixing the fringe as before and smooth everything into place with a cloth wrung out in warm water.
- Line the side of the lid in the same way.
- Paste the base circle and glue it into the bottom

4 *This ancient newspaper, which gives such an air of authenticity to my Victorian hat box, is actually a piece of modern wrapping paper. In case you are not that lucky, choose a paper in a neutral colour and with a small pattern.*

BOW

You will need:

- 1m (3ft) white curtain lining material
- Scissors
- Dressmaker's pins
- 1 reel of white cotton
- PVA glue or blind stiffener
- 2 plastic carrier bags
- 1 bottle of Poppy Red acrylic craft paint
- Brush
- Varnish

Trim off the excess material so that the strip now has a tail at either end.

of the box so that it completely covers the fringed edge of the sides and smooth with the cloth as for the lid.

- Glue the lid circle into place in the same way.
- When everything has dried out, apply one coat of sealant followed by one coat of matt varnish.

MAKING THE STIFFENED BOW

The cardboard hat boxes come in a variety of sizes so that you will have to judge exactly how large to make your bow. My box measured 30cm (12in) in diameter. For one the same size, follow these instructions.

- Cut out three pieces of material: two pieces 60 × 25cm (24 × 10in) and one piece 45 × 25cm (18 × 10in).
- Fold them all in half lengthwise and mark a point halfway along the unfolded length of each of them with a pin.
- Take one of the larger pieces and machine along one end and to within 5cm (2in) of the pin along the length. Repeat this at the other end so that you have a 10cm (4in) gap in the middle of the unfolded long side. Use this to turn the strip inside

out, before slip-stitching the gap together.

- Smooth the strip flat with your hands and mark a halfway point along the length with a pin. Fold both ends towards the middle so that they butt together at this point. Machine both ends in place so that you have a loop of material at either end.
- Repeat this process with the shorter strip and then lay the shorter bow on top of the longer one with their smooth sides outermost.
- Take the other long strip and start your machining 5cm (2in) from the middle pin. Machine straight for about 5cm (2in) and then begin to curve your stitching gradually, aiming for the far corner of the strip.
- Treat the other side in the same way, so that you again have a 10cm (4in) gap in the middle. Trim off the excess material so that your strip now has a tail at either end. Turn the strip in the right way and sew up the gap.
- Knot the tapered strip tightly around the double bow so that it covers the central stitching.

STIFFENING THE BOW

- *If you are using blind stiffener*, use it according to instructions, although if it has to be diluted, use a little less water than suggested. *If you are using glue*, dilute it with warm water, using one part glue to four parts water.
- Immerse the bow completely in the solution and wring it out thoroughly before arranging it on a board.
- Cut the carrier bags up into three or four pieces and use these to stuff the loops of the bows until they are dry. If you are feeling really artistic you can ruffle up or pleat the tails a little too. Try not to be too 'neat' with your bow . . . they look all the better for being a bit casual.
- When the bow is completely dry, remove it from the board and give it two coats of acrylic paint.
- When this is dry, give it another two coats of varnish, before gluing it on to your hat box.

Cutlery box

These sort of old cutlery boxes turn up everywhere, usually with no insides and with their veneers chipped and lifting. This one was no exception, but as I simply cannot resist reviving a lost cause, I decided to give it the works, complete with mother-of-pearl insets and a watered silk lining. The colours in the mother-of-pearl look really mouthwatering against the black background. They also complement the faded Victorian flower design, which I have allowed to tumble over the edges of the box to soften its rather hard lines.

PREPARING THE CUTLERY BOX

When I inherited this box someone had already been at it with varnish stripper, which probably accounted for the state it was in.

I had to stick down the veneer by inserting a palette knife covered in wood glue between it and the body of the box. I stood an old flat iron on this while it was drying but any heavy object would have done.

I then filled a multitude of little holes and chips with wood filler, which I rubbed down with fine sandpaper when it was dry, together with the rest of the box.

After going over the box with a tack rag (page 87) I gave it six coats of slightly thinned-down emulsion paint, lightly rubbing down and tacking every coat except the first.

DECORATING THE CUTLERY BOX

I arranged my paper cut-outs on the box and fixed them in place initially with Blu-Tack.

When I was quite happy with the design, I made a rough drawing of the box and the positions of the design pieces on it. I then put the pieces of mother-of-pearl to soak in very hot water so that they would be less brittle when I came to cut them.

I wanted to replace some of the paper details, such as leaves, flower petals and butterflies' wings with mother-of-pearl, so, taking each design piece in turn, I removed it from the box, cut off the part

I wanted to replace and then returned the remainder to the appropriate position on the box.

Using the small pieces I had cut off as templates, I laid each one on a piece of softened mother-of-pearl and cut around the shape with the scissors. I then stuck the replacement piece of mother-of-pearl back on to the design with Blu-Tack.

When I had replaced all the pieces I wanted with

1 After I had stuck down the veneer and filled all the chips and holes, the box was rubbed down and given six coats of slightly thinned-down emulsion paint (see page 81).

2 *When I had arranged the design to my satisfaction, I fixed it temporarily in place with Blu-Tack and made a rough drawing of the box so that I could re-locate the pieces later on, when the mother-of-pearl was in place.*

mother-of-pearl, I removed all the paper pieces and wrote a different letter on the back of each and on the corresponding part of the drawing.

The mother-of-pearl pieces still remained on the box and I drew around each one with a piece of chalk, before removing them one by one, gluing their backs and returning them to their places. I pressed each one down firmly with a clean fingertip and wiped off any excess glue and the chalk marks with a cloth wrung out in warm water. I then left them for several hours to dry thoroughly.

When the glue had completely dried, I gave the box another coat of black emulsion paint, removing it quickly from the mother-of-pearl with a cotton bud wrung out in warm water.

I gave the box a coat of sealant when the paint was dry, being careful, once more, to remove any traces of it from the mother-of-pearl with a cotton bud.

The box was now ready to glue the paper designs on so that they fitted around the mother-of-pearl in the correct way. This I did with the help of my drawing.

Finally, I gave the box six coats of varnish, rubbing down and tacking very carefully from the third coat onwards with a piece of fine wire wool. After each coat, I carefully removed any that had landed on the mother-of-pearl with a cotton bud wrung out in white spirit.

I then put on one last coat of varnish which I did allow to cover the entire thing, mother-of-pearl and all.

3 *Mother-of-pearl is very brittle and needs to be soaked in hot water for a minute or two, to soften it before you cut it. It cools quickly, though, so I had to keep returning it to the hot water as I worked.*

4 *Emulsion paint dries fairly quickly so I removed it from the mother-of-pearl with a cotton bud wrung out in warm water as soon as I could.*

Papier Mâché

Papier mâché, the French term which means chewed paper, describes the wonderfully simple process that transforms waste paper into a hard-wearing, hugely versatile modelling material.

The origins of papier mâché are rather obscure. It is known that the inventors of paper, the Chinese, were using pulped paper to form vessels, among other things, during the second century. It seems likely that they had found an ingenious way of recycling off-cuts of paper, which was at that time a costly and precious material. As knowledge of papermaking spread throughout the East and Europe, more countries began producing papier mâché artefacts. This tradition survives today, for example in Kashmir, where a range of exquisitely beautiful papier mâché items, including pen-holders, trays, candlesticks and boxes, is still made.

Papier mâché came into its own in Europe during the 18th century in the aftermath of the craze for chinoiserie. The popularity of imported oriental papier mâché in the west led French craftsmen to imitate the wares to satisfy local demand. Factories producing fine papier mâché furniture and decorative items sprang up in France and subsequently England. At the height of its popularity, papier mâché was used to make everything from coach panels to buttons. Many artefacts were laquered black and decorated in the oriental style with gold leaf and mother-of-pearl inlays.

Papier mâché remains a popular material in many cultures today, and is used with great enthusiasm, especially as a cheap, disposable material for carnival masks, giant figures, floats and so on. Probably the best-known papier mâché is made by the people of Mexico, whose spectacular Day of the Dead celebrations are enlivened still further by a dazzling array of grinning skeletons, leering devils and grimacing skulls, all fashioned from papier mâché.

In our environmentally-aware times, the idea of recycling unwanted rubbish into beautiful, durable objects appeals greatly. The ready availability and cheapness of the raw materials, coupled with easily-learned techniques, has led to a huge revival of interest in the medium. Artists and craftspeople alike have embraced papier mâché as an exciting, chameleon-like material that can imitate china, wood, plaster or stone, or simply be itself, a respectable alternative to more traditional materials.

▶ *An extremely versatile modelling medium, papier mâché can be used to create a wide range of beautiful objects that can imitate china, wood, plaster, stone or even metal.*

Equipment and Techniques

The beauty of papier mâche is that most of the
equipment and materials are inexpensive
and readily available – you probably already have
the basics at home.

There are only three or four basic papier mâché
techniques. Once these are learned, almost
anything is possible – all you need is
patience and practice!

Equipment and materials

THE PROCESS OF PAPIER MÂCHÉ CAN BE RATHER messy at times, especially for the novice. It is, therefore, a good idea to protect clothes with an apron and cover your work surface with a plastic sheet before you start – especially if working on a corner of the kitchen table! A gentle and domestic craft, papier mâché may sometimes call for the use of a kitchen bowl as a mould, or a cake rack to dry small items; use old equipment for this as it is not a good idea to mix craft and cookery too closely!

As you will be using glue, paint, petroleum jelly and so on, access to a sink is essential. It is amazing how quickly the hands become as sticky as fly-papers if glue is not rinsed off frequently. On average, papier mâché will need to dry for about 24 to 36 hours before it is primed and decorated. The drying process will be greatly helped if the object is placed where warm air can circulate freely around it. An airing cupboard or boiler room makes an ideal drying cabinet, but direct heat sources, such as radiators, should be avoided as they may cause the paper shape to warp.

WASTE PAPER

Almost any waste paper may be used to make papier mâché, but newspaper is the most readily available. The quality of newspaper varies greatly. Broadsheets, for example, are made with thinner, crisper newsprint than tabloids and are easier to handle once wet. It is a good idea to use alternate layers of white and coloured paper so that you can tell when you have completed each layer.

Papier mâché made from newspaper is usually painted, but attractive papers can be used to give your object an in-built surface decoration. For example, bright, handmade paper makes vibrantly coloured, very sturdy papier mâché and is especially suitable for use in moulds. Tissue paper, though rather fiddly to use, has a lovely brittle, translucent quality when dry and is especially suitable for small bowls and plates. As papier mâché is such a versatile· medium, you will probably want to experiment with different papers. Avoid those that have a waterproof or highly glossy finish, as these will be difficult to tear and stick together.

GLUE

Both PVA glue and wallpaper paste are commonly used in papier mâché. I favour PVA glue as it gives a stronger finish than paste, and dries far quicker. There are several brands of PVA glue; I use the non-toxic children's version diluted with water to the consistency of single cream. Wallpaper pastes often contain fungicide, and are not suitable for children to use, but there are non-toxic versions available. Read the manufacturer's instructions before choosing your glue; some are not suitable for constant contact with the skin. I find that a thin coat of moisturizer rubbed into the hands makes it easy to wash PVA glue off after use. Made-up wallpaper paste may be kept for several days in an airtight container. Diluted PVA glue keeps for longer.

▶*Experiment with different papers when making papier mâché. Newspaper makes a good starting point as it is readily available and cheap; for in-built decoration brightly coloured handmade paper can be used to make vibrantly coloured sturdy papier mâché.*

PETROLEUM JELLY

A thin layer of petroleum jelly rubbed over the surface of moulds, plasticine 'formers' and balloons will act as a release agent, allowing the paper shell to be removed. If a greasy film is left on the papier mâché, it may be removed by gently rubbing the area with a piece of cotton wool dipped in white spirit.

SANDPAPER

Before dry papier mâché can be primed, the surface should be gently rubbed down with fine sandpaper to give a smooth painting surface.

▼ *Rub petroleum jelly over the surface of a plasticine mould before applying papier mâché. This acts as a release agent, allowing the paper shell to be removed when dry.*

PAINTS

White matt emulsion paint makes a good, cheap primer for papier mâché. (Use a non-toxic variety.) Priming the paper gives a smooth painting surface, and prevents newsprint from showing through and spoiling the painted decoration. Some brands of paint contain more pigment than others, and cover the paper better. You will need up to three coats of primer depending on the opacity of the paint. Each coat should be allowed to dry thoroughly before the next is added, otherwise subsequent layers tend to crack and peel off. If this happens, gently sand back the paint and start again.

Acrylic gesso is more expensive than ordinary paint, but is an excellent primer for papier mâché. It gives a dense white, slightly powdery surface that is exceptionally smooth to paint on. It may also be lightly sanded to give a 'distressed' appearance that will show through a thin wash of coloured paint.

Gouache paints, poster paints and acrylic paints are useful for decorating papier mâché. I use a mixture of gouache paints and cheaper poster paints. Both these cover a surface very well, and look especially vibrant applied over a white base. Acrylic paints are also good and come in a wide range of colours. All three types of paint are water-based, although acrylics dry to a plastic finish that is waterproof, unlike the other two. Acrylic paints are especially good for paint effects such as verdigris, as they dry very quickly and may be applied on top of each other almost straightaway.

VARNISH

Varnished papier mâché is extremely strong and is also to some extent waterproof, so pieces may be wiped clean with a damp cloth. I use clear gloss polyurethane wood varnish because my paints are

water-based. Two or three coats give a glassy, extremely durable finish. Water-based acrylic or craft varnishes should only be used on waterproof paints, as they will make gouache and poster paints run. Slightly dilute PVA glue makes a good varnish; it dries clear, but again should only be used on waterproof paints. All varnishes start to yellow with time – polyurethane wood varnishes more than other types.

MOULDS
I have used all sorts of objects as moulds, including plates, bowls, trays and cake tins. One golden rule should be observed when selecting a mould – there should be no undercuts, that is no part of the mould should extend further than the opening through which the paper shell is to be removed. If this rule is not observed, it will be impossible to remove the paper once it has dried in the mould. A thin

▲ *Gouache, poster and acrylic paints are all useful for decorating papier mâché. All three types of paint are water based.*

layer of petroleum jelly should be smeared around the mould before it is used, to release the papier mâché easily. I prefer to apply paper to the *inside* of a mould rather than the outside, as the paper is prone to split otherwise when it dries and contracts. Excellent moulds or 'formers' may be made from plastic modelling clay (plasticine) and balloons. These should be smeared with petroleum jelly before being covered with papier mâché in the usual way.

CARDBOARD

Corrugated cardboard makes a good, solid armature or base to which papier mâché may be applied. It is especially useful for making frames and boxes, as the cardboard remains inside the papier mâché as an integral part of the object, giving it strength. Corrugated card comes in several thicknesses. The most suitable is of double wall construction, that is, with two rows of corrugations.

CRAFT KNIFE AND CUTTING BOARD

A craft knife and metal ruler are very useful for cutting heavy cardboard. There are several types of knife available; the easiest to use are scalpels, which have detachable blades. Those with swivel heads are also good, especially for cutting intricate designs. A cutting board is essential when using a craft knife. A simple one may be made from an offcut of plywood, or you can invest in a more expensive plastic version from an art supplier's.

BRUSHES

A selection of brushes will be needed for priming, decorating and varnishing your papier mâché. Ordinary house-painting brushes are fine for applying primer and varnish. Buy the best quality that you can afford, as really cheap brushes

constantly shed hair, giving a poor surface finish. Painted decoration should be applied with artist's paintbrushes, picked to suit the type of paint you are using. Sable brushes are excellent for gouache and poster paints but are often prohibitively expensive. However, there are good nylon or nylon and hair alternatives available. Acrylic paints should be applied with thicker, stronger brushes that will stand up to more vigorous washing.

MASKING TAPE

Masking tape is a removable paper tape which is very useful for holding the joints of cardboard armatures together while papier mâché is applied.

◄◄ *All sorts of objects can be used as moulds for papier mâché, including bowls, plates and even cake tins.*

▲ *You will need a range of brushes for priming, decorating and varnishing your papier mâché.*

Basic techniques

▼ When covering small, fiddly pieces of card with papier mâché, it is best to use small, thin strips of paper so you retain the definition of the shape.

THE SECRET OF REALLY PROFESSIONAL-LOOKING papier mâché is attention to detail. Care should be taken to apply the layers of paper neatly and evenly to get a smooth finish, and careful sanding and priming make all the difference. As with all things, new skills need practice, and very pleasing results may be obtained with a little perseverance.

Papier mâché may be divided into two groups: that made by layering strips of paper, and the kind made from soaked, pulped paper. I use strips of newspaper to make mine; experiments with pulp have convinced me that life is too short to boil waste paper! However, pulped paper objects have a grainy pitted surface that I like very much, so I occasionally use cleaned, dehydrated pulp that may be bought from educational suppliers and some craft shops. This material can be rehydrated with a little water to make a spongy mass which I squeeze dry and mix with glue and a filler such as sawdust. The resulting papier mâché may be pressed into a greased mould in the usual way or used like clay to build all sorts of objects.

PAPIER MÂCHÉ STRIPS

I make papier mâché by the layering method, where strips of newspaper are laid on top of each other to build up a shape. The length and width of the strips I make depend on what I want to use them for. Large flat objects, such as plates, may be formed from strips as wide as 7.5cm (3in), while I find it most practical to cover fiddly pieces such as intricate frames with small, thin strips. You will quickly discover what is most practical for you. Moulds should be filled with strips that are slightly too long so that they overlap the edge. This will ensure that all the mould is covered. The rough edges may be trimmed back to the rim with scissors. Newspaper has a definite grain, and will tear much more easily in one direction than the other – it will be obvious which is the right way! The paper should always be torn and never cut. Papier mâché made from cut strips has hard, ugly edges that spoil the appearance of the work.

APPLYING GLUE

Whether you use wallpaper paste or diluted PVA glue, it should be of a smooth, fairly thin consistency, something like single cream. Some craftspeople glue their newspaper strips with a

◄ For low-relief decoration, glue paper pulp pellets onto an object. They are made by rolling a gluey strip of paper into a small ball between finger and thumb. They can be covered with small strips of paper for a smooth surface.

▼ When covering large flat objects such as plates with papier mâché, use wide strips of paper and lay down each layer in alternating directions, first lengthwise and then crosswise, for extra strength.

paintbrush, but I prefer to apply the glue with my hands. If you don't like the feel of the glue or have sensitive skin, you could try wearing very thin rubber surgical gloves! It is important not to saturate the paper strips with glue as they will disintegrate as they are applied to moulds, and can also warp cardboard armatures. If you do apply too much glue, you can soak up the excess by dabbing the surface with a sponge.

PULP ADDITIONS

Low-relief decorative details may be added to a papier mâché object with paper pulp pellets. These are made by rolling a gluey strip of newspaper into a small ball between finger and thumb. The pellets may be stuck directly to the papier mâché in the required shape and covered with small strips of paper to give a smooth surface.

APPLYING STRIPS

Glued paper strips should be applied to a cardboard base or placed in a mould in alternating directions to ensure strong papier mâché. The first layer of paper should run from top to bottom, and the second from side to side, at right angles to the first, rather like woven cloth. Each strip should slightly overlap the preceding one for extra strength. As each layer is completed, smooth the papier mâché with your fingers to push out any air bubbles.

DRYING TIMES

Drying time varies according to the number of layers applied and the type of glue used. PVA glue dries more quickly than wallpaper paste – often overnight if applied to a cardboard armature.

Mould-made items generally take longer – the papier mâché can usually be removed after 24 to 36 hours, then turned upside-down so both sides are dried thoroughly. Ideally papier mâché should be dried in freely circulating warm air. In cold, damp weather, it will take longer. A cake rack is indispensible for drying objects on, as air can flow underneath, thus speeding up the process.

BINDING CUT EDGES

Once mould-made items are dry, the ragged edges should be trimmed and bound. Binding prevents the layers of papier mâché separating during

▲ *Once a mould-made item is dry, trim the ragged edge and then bind it with small thin strips of paper wrapped over the cut edge to neaten it.*

▶ *When the papier mâché object is dry, rub it gently with fine sandpaper both before and after priming to achieve a really good, smooth finish.*

painting and varnishing. Small, thin strips should be glued, wrapped over the cut edge, and torn off at the other side.

SANDING

To ensure a really good finish, dry papier mâché should be smoothed with fine sandpaper before and after priming. Never use coarse sandpaper, as it may pit the surface of your work with small craters!

APPLYING ADDITIONS

Additions such as handles may be cut from heavy corrugated cardboard and added to the main papier mâché shape. The cardboard should be primed first with dilute PVA glue and allowed to dry thoroughly. This will prevent it from warping too much, if at all, when the papier mâché is applied. Additions should be stuck to the papier mâché with strong clear glue and the joints held firm with strips of masking tape while they dry.

BASES AND NECKS

Yogurt pots and plastic tubs make good bases and necks for vases, bowls and so on. They should first be cleaned and dried, then stuck to the papier mâché with PVA glue and held in place with masking

▲ *Attach extra card pieces such as handles to the main papier mâché shape using strong glue and hold the joints firm with masking tape. The tape can be left in position for extra strength.*

◄ *To make bases and necks for vases and bowls, cut off the base of a cleaned and dried yogurt pot and attach a length of cord around the rim to make a lip.*

tape. The plastic can be covered with papier mâché in the usual way; PVA glue is best for this as it adheres more readily to the surface than wallpaper paste.

▼ To construct a cardboard armature, first join each section together with glue and then hold the joints firm with strips of masking tape.

ARMATURES

Each section of cardboard armature should be glued together with glue, and the joints held firm with masking tape while they dry. The masking tape can then either be removed or left in position to give the armature extra strength. Before papier

mâché is applied, the armature should be primed with a coat of dilute PVA glue and allowed to dry to prevent warping.

PLASTICINE FORMERS

Plasticine formers should be greased with petroleum jelly before applying papier mâché. Once dry, cut it open with a craft knife and prise the two halves from the plasticine. Then the paper shells should be glued, re-joined and sealed with strips of papier mâché.

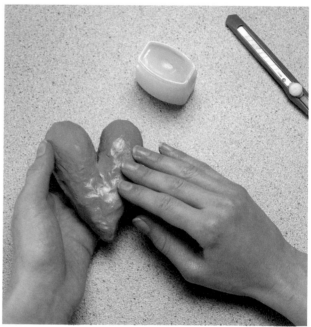

▲ Grease a plasticine former or mould thoroughly with petroleum jelly before applying papier mâché strips. The petroleum jelly acts as a release agent, enabling the papier mâché to be removed when it is dry.

◄ *When the papier mâché is dry, carefully cut it open around the edge with a craft knife. Then gently prise the two halves from the plasticine. If any of the plasticine sticks to the paper shell, simply scrape it off with a spoon.*

▼ *Using PVA glue, paste the two paper shell halves back together again and hold in place with small pieces of masking tape. When dry, conceal the join by pasting small thin strips of papier mâché all around the glued and taped edge.*

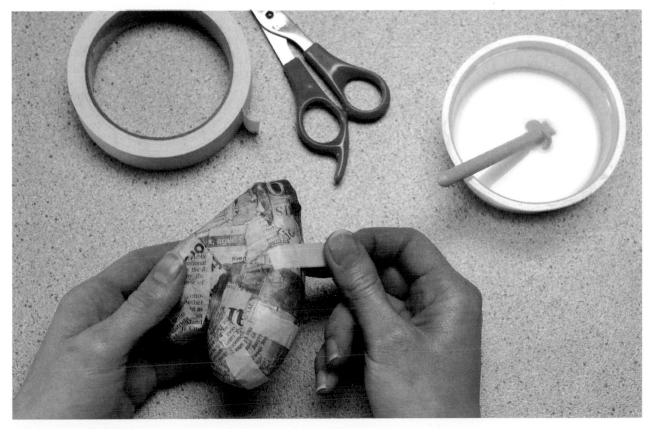

Projects

There is a vast range of delightful objects that you can make with papier mâché. The projects that follow include a clock, a mirror frame, a vase, a selection of jewellery and a decorative plate. But these are simply suggestions – hopefully you will be inspired to go on and develop your own creative ideas.

Clock

This witty clock, simply constructed from a cardboard armature, would enliven any mantelpiece. Decorate your clock in a colour scheme to match your decor, or go wild and produce a multi-coloured clock that would certainly not go unnoticed.

You will need:
- Metal ruler
- Pencil
- Corrugated card
- Set square
- Cutting board
- Craft knife
- Ballpoint pen
- PVA glue or cellulose paste
- Masking tape
- Newspaper
- Fine sandpaper
- White primer
- Paintbrushes
- Acrylic paint
- Scissors
- Handmade paper in bright colours
- Clock movement and hands
- Acrylic varnish

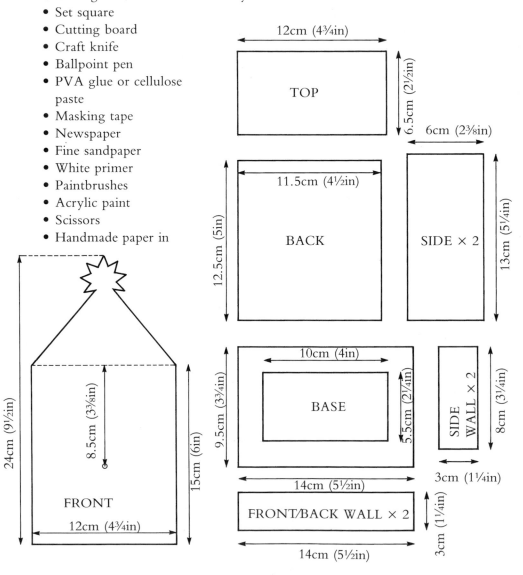

12cm (4¾in)

TOP

6.5cm (2½in)

6cm (2⅜in)

11.5cm (4½in)

12.5cm (5in)

BACK

SIDE × 2

13cm (5¼in)

10cm (4in)

9.5cm (3¾in)

BASE

5.5cm (2¼in)

SIDE WALL × 2

8cm (3¼in)

14cm (5½in)

3cm (1¼in)

FRONT/BACK WALL × 2

3cm (1¼in)

14cm (5½in)

24cm (9½in)

8.5cm (3⅜in)

15cm (6in)

FRONT

12cm (4¾in)

1 Following the diagram, measure and mark up each piece of clock on corrugated card using a set square, pencil and ruler. Place the card on a cutting board, and carefully cut around each piece of armature with a craft knife, cutting against the metal ruler for straight edges. Make a hole at the correct position in the front of the clock with a ballpoint pen so that the movement may be fitted. Assemble the armature using strong PVA glue and strips of masking tape to hold the joints firm. Depending on the thickness of the cardboard you use, you may have to trim some sections slightly as you work to ensure a close fit. Leave the masking tape in place even when the glue has dried, as this will give strength to the structure. Prime the armature with a coat of watered-down PVA glue and leave it to dry.

2 Cover the clock with five layers of papier mâché strips (you won't be able to cover all of the inside). Use small, thin pieces of paper to cover the star at the top of the armature. Remember not to paper over the hole for the clock movement! Let the clock dry thoroughly, then lightly sand it and then prime it with two coats of white paint. Allow the paint to dry then apply a coat of acrylic paint for the base colour.

3 Cut out squares and triangles of brightly coloured handmade paper and use them to decorate the clock. Apply each piece of paper with a dab of PVA glue. Cut a circle of coloured paper and stick it to the front of the clock over the hole to make the face. Before the paper dries, renew the hole by pushing a ballpoint pen through it.

4 Following the manufacturer's instructions, fit the movement to the front of the clock and attach the hands. Gently push the hands around and lightly mark each hour on the face. Use thin strips or triangles of paper to mark the divisions. When the clock is dry, remove the clock movement before sealing the clock with two coats of acrylic varnish. Then replace the movement as before.

Mirror frame

Created from layers of corrugated card, this fishy mirror frame is ideal for hanging on a bathroom wall, or standing on a shelf. If you would prefer a larger mirror in which to admire your reflection, simply increase the amount of card accordingly.

You will need:

- Metal ruler
- Pencil
- Corrugated card
- Set square
- Cutting board
- Craft knife
- PVA glue or cellulose paste
- Masking tape
- 4 cotton reels
- Newspaper
- Fine sandpaper
- White primer
- Paintbrushes
- Gouache or poster paints
- Waterproof black ink
- Clear gloss polyurethane varnish
- Mirror tile
- Metal plate and D-ring hangers and chain

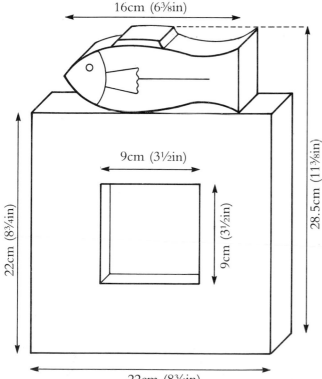

16cm (6⅜in)

9cm (3½in)

9cm (3½in)

22cm (8¾in)

28.5cm (11⅜in)

22cm (8¾in)

1 Following the diagram, measure and mark up the front and back of the frame onto corrugated card using a set square, pencil and ruler. Place the card on a cutting board and carefully cut out the pieces with a craft knife, using a metal ruler for straight edges. Paste PVA glue onto the reverse of the frame front and stick the front and back together. Hold the join together with strips of masking tape. Let the glue dry for an hour or so, then seal the frame with a coat of diluted PVA glue and lay it flat to dry. Support each corner with a cotton reel, or similar, to allow the air to circulate underneath the frame.

2 Using 2.5cm (1in) wide strips of newspaper, cover the frame with four layers of papier mâché. You will need smaller strips to go around the fish. Push the paper well into the corners of the frame opening to leave a neat space for the mirror tile. Allow the frame to dry thoroughly, and then sand it lightly and prime it with two coats of white paint. Draw in the fish's features and border design with a pencil.

3 Fill in the fish designs using gouache or poster paints. You will probably have to apply two coats to get a good, deep colour. Allow the paint to dry thoroughly and then accentuate the design with waterproof black ink. Seal the finished frame with two coats of clear gloss varnish. Stick the mirror tile in place onto the front of the frame, using strong clear glue. Attach two D-ring hangers to the back of the frame.

Vase

This two-handled vase is made from one of the best-loved papier mâché techniques, and one that can be the most fun – layering over a balloon. But take care not to be too heavy handed – remember that balloons are not indestructible!

You will need:
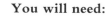
- Round balloon
- Shallow basin
- Petroleum jelly
- Newspaper
- PVA glue or cellulose paste
- String
- Pin
- 2 plastic cheese tubs, washed and dried
- Scissors
- Masking tape
- Pencil
- Cotton cord
- Corrugated card
- Craft knife
- Cutting board
- Paintbrushes
- Fine sandpaper
- White primer
- Acrylic paint
- Small piece of natural sponge
- Matt acrylic varnish

1 Blow up the balloon and tie the end tightly. Place the balloon in a shallow basin so that it is supported while you cover it. Grease the surface of the balloon with petroleum jelly. Tear 2.5cm (1in) strips of newspaper and cover the balloon with six layers of papier mâché. Attach a length of string to the end of the balloon and suspend it where it can hang freely (from the edge of a shelf, for example) while it dries.

2 When the surface of the papier mâché feels dry (after about two or three days), push a pin through the paper to pop the balloon, and pull it out. To make the neck and foot of the vase, take two clean plastic cheese tubs, one slightly larger than the other. Carefully cut the base from each using scissors. Smear a little PVA glue around the cut edge of the larger tub. Position the narrow end of the balloon so that it sits straight on the tub and hold it in position with masking tape to form the foot of the vase. Cut the base from the smaller tub and place it on the top of the balloon, in the centre. Draw around the inside of the tub onto the papier mâché. Carefully cut out the resulting circle to make an opening. Glue and tape the tub in position over the opening to make the neck. Glue a length of cotton cord around the foot and neck to make more substantial rims.

3 Cut a pair of handles from corrugated card. Stick them in position on the side of the vase with PVA glue. Hold them in place with strips of masking tape. Then prime the handles with dilute PVA glue and allow to dry before covering with papier mâché.

4 Cover the neck, foot and handles with three layers of papier mâché. When the vase is dry, lightly sand the surface, and prime with two coats of white paint. Paint the vase with a coat of dark green acrylic paint and allow to dry. Using a piece of natural sponge, gently dab light turquoise-green paint on top of the first coat in a broken pattern to emulate verdigris. Add white highlights if desired. Seal the whole vase with two coats of matt acrylic varnish.

Plate

Although not advisable to eat off it, this elegantly decorated plate would look lovely displayed on a sideboard, or used as a receptacle for fruit, sweets or nuts. Once you have mastered layering over a mould, try experimenting with different vessels, such as bowls and cake tins for more unusual papier mâché creations.

You will need:
- China plate
- Petroleum jelly
- Newspaper
- PVA glue or cellulose paste
- Blunt knife
- Scissors
- Fine sandpaper
- White primer
- Gouache, poster or acrylic paint
- Paintbrushes
- Varnish

1 Cover the china plate with a thin coat of petroleum jelly. Using paper strips approximately 4cm (1½in) wide and slightly longer than the plate, apply the first layer of papier mâché, overlapping each strip slightly. The second layer should run in the opposite direction at right angles to the first. Apply a total of six layers of papier mâché.

2 Allow the papier mâché to dry thoroughly, then remove it from the mould by slipping the blade of a blunt knife between the mould and the paper and easing the paper plate away.

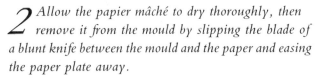

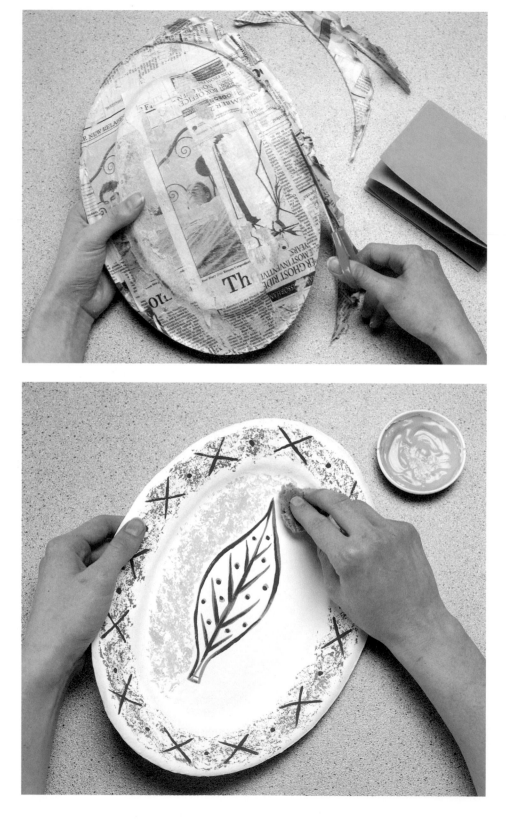

3 *Trim the rough edges back to the rim of the shape and sand until smooth. Bind the cut edges with small, thin strips of papier mâché.*

4 *Apply two coats of white paint and leave to dry. Then decorate the plate, using gouache, poster or acrylic paint and leave to dry. Finally, varnish the plate to seal.*

Jewellery

Making your own papier mâché earrings and brooches gives you the opportunity to be truly creative. Once you have exhausted the possibilities of paints, sequins and silk, try decorating your jewellery with beads, foil and even sweet wrappers!

You will need:
- Pencil
- Thin corrugated card
- Ruler
- Scissors
- PVA glue or cellulose paste
- Paintbrushes
- Newspaper
- Fine sandpaper
- White primer
- Gold poster paint
- Scraps of brightly coloured silk
- Coloured sequins
- Strong clear glue
- Brooch fastening
- Earring clips

1 Draw irregular rectangles onto thin corrugated card. The brooch should measure approximately 6.5 × 2.5cm (2¼ × 1in), and the earrings 4 × 2.5cm (1¼ × 1in). Cut out the shapes and seal them with a coat of diluted PVA glue. Allow them to dry, then cover with three layers of small, thin papier mâché strips. Lightly sand the dry papier mâché, and prime with two coats of white paint.

2 Paint the prepared shapes with gold paint. Cut and fray scraps of brightly coloured silk. Stick them to one side of each piece of jewellery. Stick coloured sequins on top using strong clear glue. Then stick brooch fastenings and earring clips to the back of the jewellery.

Index